The Grand Canyon

THE GRAND CANYON

intimate views

Edited by

Robert C. Euler & Frank Tikalsky

With a Foreword by Ann H. Zwinger

The University of Arizona Press / TUCSON & LONDON

The University of Arizona Press

Copyright © 1992 by Frank D. Tikalsky and Robert C. Euler
All rights reserved

Printed in Hong Kong

97 96 95 94 93 92   6 5 4 3 2 1

Library of Congress Cataloging-in-Publication Data

The Grand Canyon : intimate views / edited by Robert C. Euler and Frank
    Tikalsky : with a foreword by Ann H. Zwinger.
        p.   cm.
    Includes bibliographical references.
    ISBN 0-8165-1295-7 (pbk.)
    1. Grand Canyon (Ariz.)—History.   2. Grand Canyon (Ariz.)—
Description and travel—Guide-books.   3. Natural history—Arizona—
Grand Canyon.   I. Euler, Robert C.   II. Tikalsky, Frank D.
F788.G747   1992   91-32187
979.1′32—dc20   CIP

British Cataloguing-in-Publication Data
A catalogue record for this book is available from the British Library.

CONTENTS

FIGURES

FOREWORD

I first went down the Colorado River in the Grand Canyon in May of 1976, just after writing a book on the Green River, during which time I had studiously avoided running the Colorado River because I didn't want to lose focus, didn't want to be overwhelmed by this massive canyon, this overpowering river. When that book was over and published, I wanted to complete my time of river running with the ultimate: the Colorado River in the Grand Canyon, sure that I would write no more river books, do no more river trips, and this rowing trip would be the grand finale (so to speak), the *ne plus ultra*.

Now, thirteen years later, after saying I would never run Lava Falls again, I am writing about the natural history of the Colorado River in the Grand Canyon, or what happens to a big river when you put a big dam on it. The Grand Canyon is rich and complex, a place that catches not only the eye but the heart. People who love it, love it passionately.

I am overwhelmed by a grandeur that goes on and on without respite—there is a lot of it to react to: 279 miles, if you go the whole distance, too much of a muchness. But as time goes

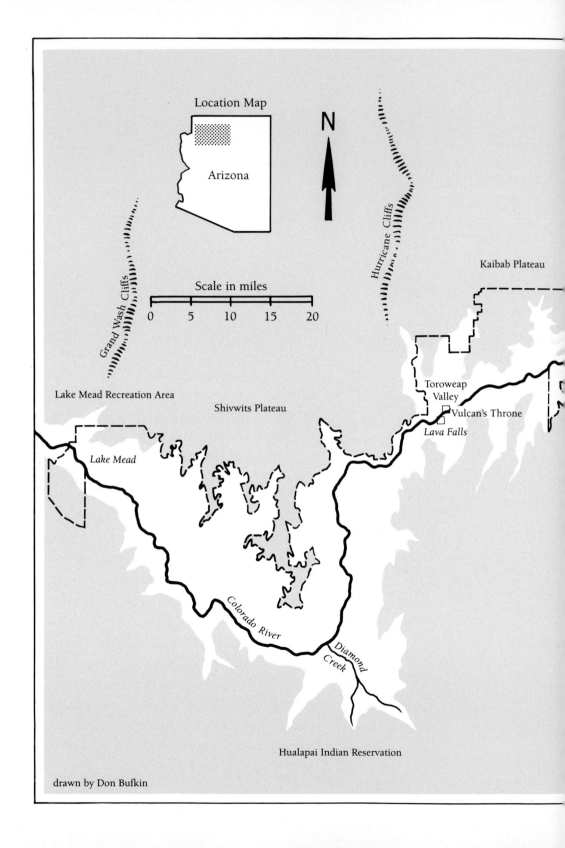

Location Map

Arizona

N

Grand Wash Cliffs

Hurricane Cliffs

Kaibab Plateau

Scale in miles

0   5   10   15   20

Lake Mead Recreation Area

Shivwits Plateau

Toroweap Valley

Vulcan's Throne

Lava Falls

Lake Mead

Colorado River

Diamond Creek

Hualapai Indian Reservation

drawn by Don Bufkin

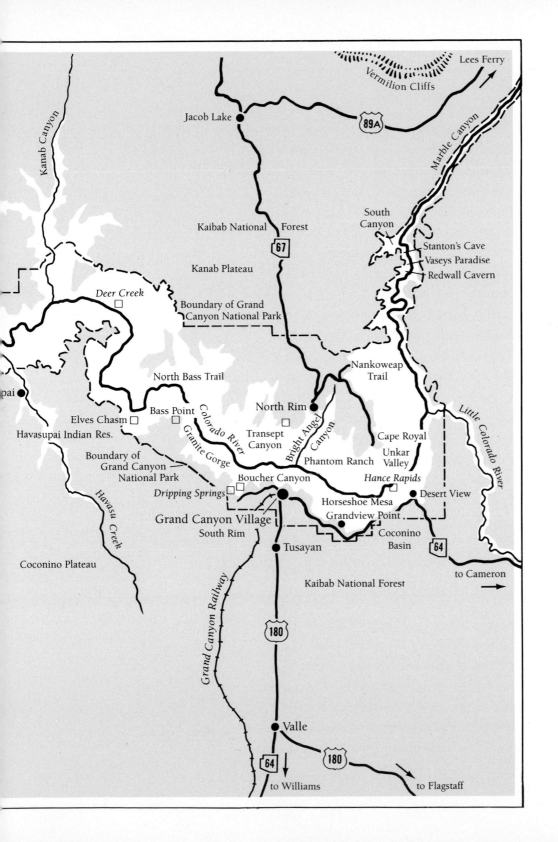

Lees Ferry

Vermilion Cliffs

Jacob Lake

89A

Marble Canyon

Kanab Canyon

Kaibab National   Forest

South
Canyon

Stanton's Cave
Vaseys Paradise
Redwall Cavern

67

Kanab Plateau

Deer Creek

Boundary of Grand
Canyon National Park

Nankoweap
Trail

North Bass Trail

Little Colorado River

pai

Bass Point

Colorado River

North Rim

Elves Chasm

Transept
Canyon

Bright Angel   Canyon

Cape Royal

Havasupai Indian Res.

Granite Gorge

Phantom Ranch

Unkar
Valley

Boundary of
Grand Canyon
National Park

Hance Rapids

Dripping Springs

Boucher Canyon

Desert View

Grand Canyon Village

Horseshoe Mesa
Grandview Point

South Rim

Coconino Basin

64

Havasu Creek

Tusayan

Coconino Plateau

Kaibab National Forest

to Cameron

Grand Canyon Railway

180

Valle

64

180

to Williams

to Flagstaff

by, I find I also have an affection, a deep commitment, an intense involvement in the river and its issues. My advantage is that I can come back again and again. And in so doing I begin to watch for the landslide at river mile 10 that says Badger Rapid is around the corner, know the perfect place at Shinumo to throw my sleeping bag, see if the coccinid bugs are still on the prickly pear at the South Canyon Anasazi site, recognize from a distance the thin point of land at Nankoweap Creek where I spent a January week bald eagle watching, feel glad I don't have to get off at Phantom Ranch, look forward to the jointed basalt columns around Lava Falls, and pass Kanab Creek and Separation Canyon with a better understanding of Major John Wesley Powell's tribulations.

Realizing how much repeated time in the Canyon means in coming to know it gives me a healthy respect and admiration for these authors, each of whom is on a personal footing with the Canyon, not only because of years of research into their chosen subjects but because they have seen it on foot, from the river, even from a helicopter. None of them is a desktop scholar who never sees nature except through a window. All are dedicated, experienced, and knowledgeable hands in the Grand Canyon, out there with scratches and squint lines and a love of place that pulls them back again and again.

Stanley Beus has tramped the miles and climbed the cliffs that give his geological insights particular validity. He also writes with clarity and conciseness. Bob Euler is the adored mentor of many Grand Canyon archaeologists, a man who through time has sifted and puzzled and sweated through excavations of dozens of sites. Steve Carothers, the enthusiastic biologist, has studied the creatures that skitter and flee and watch with wary eyes, has looked at the plants with hairs and

Preceding pages: The Grand Canyon

thorns and delicate flowers, and has put together an essay that is a joy to read. Frank Tikalsky has given an expert and succinct introduction to hiking, based on many hours and many miles hoisting up and down those formidable canyon walls. Kim Crumbo, a riverman and national park ranger, provides a devoted, delightful, and thoughtful history of river running.

Enhancing their clean, clear words are handsome color and black-and-white photographs that illuminate the Canyon's essence. Together they have produced a book that is more than the sum of its parts, that gives the reader a new appreciation, in the fullest sense of the word, of the Grand Canyon. They point out quietly and without fanfare what must be done to ensure that it be healthy. We—you and I and whoever follows this river and whoever may never even see it—are responsible for the care of this magnificent part of the American West, this unique part of our United States, this irreplaceable, irreproducible combination of whiptail lizard and seething rapid, gray rock walls stained red and caverned, red shale slopes buttoned with barrel cactus, opulent datura blossoms, and haughty desert bighorn sheep. They make us aware that time in the Canyon is more than a quick picture-taking opportunity. The Grand Canyon requires and deserves our dedication and commitment to its health and continued welfare. It is our responsibility to keep it wind-open and running free.

ANN H. ZWINGER
November 1990

ACKNOWLEDGMENTS

The editors express their gratitude to Demila Jenner for her editorial suggestions, to Lawrence Leith for initially proofreading the manuscript, to Linda Kakuk Holschbach for her many hours of typing, and to Don Bufkin for his fine map of the Canyon.

INTRODUCTION

This book was written for students and visitors—whether
viewing the Canyon from its rims, hiking its trails, or running
the river. It also recognizes the need to learn more about the
Canyon's infinite variety and to comprehend the fragility of its
environment. This series of essays written by scholars and scientific researchers is a labor of love dedicated to the idea that
the Canyon's magnificence must be preserved for present and
future generations to enjoy.

The various authors presented here have infused their writing with the accumulated knowledge garnered through un-
counted hours of boat and helicopter travel, a thousand-plus
miles of canyon hiking, and measureless hours of contempla-
tion. Few books ever published about the Grand Canyon can
claim such a vast and comprehensive study, such a distillation
of its wonder.

Thus, while this guide grew from scholarly input, the reflec-
tion of intimate awareness and understanding of the Canyon
is its most important feature. We feel this is the way we can
best illustrate how joyous the canyon experience can be while

simultaneously warning of the sometimes-destructive impact of human visitation on its well-being.

This book is an enlarged and updated edition, with two entirely new chapters, of *The Grand Canyon: Up Close and Personal,* first published in 1980. Many of the illustrations reproduced here were included in the original edition, and unless otherwise noted, the photographs are by Robert Euler. So what more can we tell you? Read. Learn. Enjoy!

Robert C. Euler
Frank Tikalsky

The Grand Canyon

1 / *The Geologic Record*

STANLEY S. BEUS

*I*t can be a humbling experience to descend to the canyon floor and stand among ancient rocks: they speak of a time eons before humans appeared, when the earth was young and nearly barren of life, when the crust of North America was just being formed. The twisted and contorted bands of the oldest rocks along the Inner Gorge are probably the roots of an ancient mountain system that once stood miles high near the edge of our primeval continent.

The rocks and landscapes of the Grand Canyon present a marvelous revelation of the earth's history perhaps unmatched elsewhere on the surface of our planet. The exposed record spans nearly 2 billion years beginning with the formation of the oldest "basement rocks" of the Inner Gorge and continuing with the canyon excavation in progress.

From selected viewpoints on the South Rim of the eastern Grand Canyon a visitor can see in one view outcrops of four great groups of rock: (1) the metamorphic and igneous rock complex of the Inner Gorge, (2) the tilted stack of sedimentary layers called the Grand Canyon Supergroup, (3) the horizontal stack of Paleozoic sedimentary rocks forming the upper 4,000 feet of the canyon walls, and in the distance to the east, (4) the escarpments and mesas of Mesozoic strata that once covered the Grand Canyon region. Small isolated remnants of the latter still perch along the canyon rim.

The oldest rocks are best exposed along the thousand-foot walls of the Inner Gorge between Hance Rapids (about river mile 77) and Elves Chasm (near mile 117). These rocks are the greenish-black schist of the Vishnu Metamorphic Complex, associated with smaller pods of lighter granite gneiss and intrusions of pink or white granite of the Zoroaster Plutonic Complex. Deep burial and prolonged pressure formed the Vishnu by metamorphosing the original sedimentary and volcanic rocks into mica-rich schist and gneiss. The granite records the cooling and crystallizing of magma (molten rock material) that formed deep in the crust of the earth and was injected into the Vishnu about 1.7 billion years ago. The Vishnu is clearly older than the intruding granite: exactly how old we may never know but probably on the order of 2 billion years.

Following the deformation and uplift of the Vishnu, erosion wore down and removed most of these rocks and produced a nearly level plain in the Grand Canyon region at the western edge of North America. About 1.2 billion years ago shallow seas began periodically flooding across this plain, and deposits of sand and silt (and locally, lime mud) buried the old erosion surface. That buried surface, called the great unconformity by John Wesley Powell, sharply truncates the Vishnu and represents, as do all unconformities, a time of erosion and nondeposition, in this case nearly half a billion years of time!

The strata above the great unconformity constitute the Grand Canyon Supergroup and are best exposed in the big bend area

Facing page 1: View to the North Rim from Hopi Point

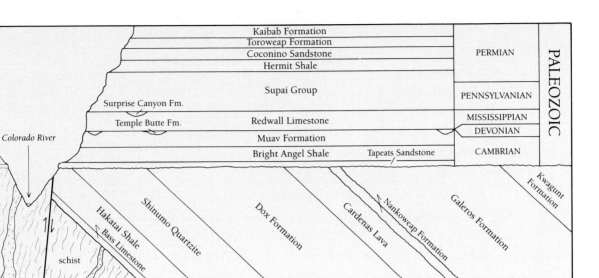

Kaibab Formation			
Toroweap Formation	PERMIAN	PALEOZOIC
Coconino Sandstone		
Hermit Shale		
Supai Group	PENNSYLVANIAN	
Surprise Canyon Fm.		
Temple Butte Fm. Redwall Limestone	MISSISSIPPIAN	
	DEVONIAN	
Muav Formation	CAMBRIAN	
Bright Angel Shale Tapeats Sandstone		

Colorado River

Hakatai Shale
Bass Limestone
Shinumo Quartzite
Dox Formation
Cardenas Lava
Nankoweap Formation
Galeros Formation
Kwagunt Formation

schist

granite

Unkar Group   Chuar Group

EARLY PROTEROZOIC   MIDDLE PROTEROZOIC

Geologic strata of the Grand Canyon

of the eastern Grand Canyon between river mile 64 (Lees Ferry is mile 0) and Hance Rapids. More than 12,000 feet of sedimentary rocks form the Supergroup and record deposition on deltas, on tidal flats, and in shallow marine environments during the Proterozoic Era (about 1.2 to 0.8 billion years ago). At the top of the Unkar Group strata, which make up the lower half of the supergroup, is an 800-foot-thick section of basaltic lava flows, the Cardenas Lava, which have been radiometrically dated to about 1.1 billion years ago.

Limestone and dolomite layers in the Grand Canyon Supergroup contain some gently arched or hemispherical fossils called stromatolites—some the size and shape of a cabbage head—formed by blue-green algae in tidal flats or shallow marine environments. These oldest traces of life in the Grand Canyon closely resemble the oldest traces of life found anywhere on earth, such as those in rocks of Africa that are nearly 3.5 billion years old. The Grand Canyon stromatolites are most extensively preserved in the Bass Limestone, the basal formation of the Supergroup, and in the Kwagunt Formation of the Chuar Group (exposed only in Chuar Valley north and west of the Colorado River at the big bend).

In late Proterozoic time the strata of the Grand Canyon Supergroup were uplifted and broken by faults into a series of tilted blocks with long slopes and steep escarpments much like the present-day mountain blocks of Nevada. Another prolonged episode of erosion reduced these mountain blocks, making the tallest only 800 feet. Another great unconformity separates with angular discordance the tilted Proterozoic strata beneath from the younger horizontal Paleozoic strata above.

Soon after the beginning of the Paleozoic era, some 570 million years ago, shallow seas again flooded slowly across northern Arizona from west to east. The lowest deposits of this Cambrian-period marine transgression are the gravel and sand of the Tapeats Sandstone. These sediments grade upward into the Bright Angel Shale and still higher into the Muav Limestone and record the shallow sea having moved eastward across the interior of the continent, depositing sediments as it went.

The fossil record is suddenly richer and more clear, for by this time a multitude of different animals such as trilobites and brachiopods, with hard preservable exoskeletons, had appeared. In addition, a variety of mostly unknown creatures left strange crawling, feeding, and burrowing traces in the soft mud of the sea floor. These trace fossils are now extensively preserved in the Bright Angel Shale of the Grand Canyon.

Angular unconformity in the
Grand Canyon Supergroup (Photograph by Stanley Beus)

One hundred forty million years of erosion or nondeposition followed the Cambrian deposition record, and this pattern of gentle subsidence and deposition followed by gentle uplift and mild erosion occurred repeatedly through much of the Paleozoic and Mesozoic eras in northern Arizona. The rock and fossil record of the Paleozoic portion of those episodes is richly preserved in the upper 4,000 feet of the canyon wall. The widespread layers of the Redwall Limestone and adjacent formations of the same age record shallow marine conditions in a sea that extended from Canada to Mexico across the western interior of North America and swarmed with corals, lacy bryozoans,

Trace fossils in the Bright Angel Shale (Photograph by Stanley Beus)

brachiopods, crinoids, and other invertebrate animals as well as algae, sharks, and fish. The equally fossiliferous but narrowly restricted Surprise Canyon Formation above the Redwall indicates that these marine creatures lived in a long, narrow estuary across the Grand Canyon region.

The layers forming the upper 2,000 feet of the canyon wall record even more dramatic variations in environment, from sea to desert. Thus, the redbeds of the Supai Group and Hermit Shale indicate marginal marine to coastal plain conditions (and locally, coastal swamps). The bright yellowish-gray Coconino Sandstone records the spread of windblown sand dunes across

Arizona for several million years, with tracks of four-footed reptiles or amphibians often seen on the dunes.

The uppermost two formations, the Toroweap and Kaibab, record another two major transgressions and regressions of the sea, culminating in the fossiliferous limestone deposits of the Kaibab Formation, the rimrock of the Grand Canyon. The end of the Paleozoic record is marked by yet another major unconformity—an erosion surface representing about 15 million years—between the top of the Kaibab Formation and the base of the overlying redbeds of the Moenkopi Formation of the Triassic Period, seen to the north and east of the Grand Canyon.

The Moenkopi and later formations dominate the landscape of northern Arizona and southern Utah in a series of colorful cliffs and mesas that resemble giant stairs, composed of alternating resistant beds—the treads—and less resistant layers—the risers. They are the retreating remnants of the great Mesozoic "sandpile" together with shale, conglomerate, and limestone that accumulated under a variety of conditions from about 240 to 50 million years ago. They must once have covered the Grand Canyon region, since remnants occur along the canyon rim as small patches or isolated buttes. These strata and rocks of equivalent age elsewhere preserved the entire paleontological record of the so-called age of reptiles, when dinosaurs ruled the earth for more than 100 million years.

Some of these layers were conveniently naturally color coded, as witnessed by the names applied by earlier travelers who kept a slower and more observing pace across this monumental landscape. Thus, the Shinarump Conglomerate forms the Chocolate Cliffs, and the orangish-red sandstone beds of the Moenave and Kayenta formations form the Vermilion Cliffs.

The light gray cross-bedded sandstones of the Navajo Sandstone are the White Cliffs where the great towers of Zion National Park occur. At Bryce Canyon National Park, high on the plateaus of southern Utah, are the Pink Cliffs of the Cenozoic-age Wasatch Formation.

By the time of the Wasatch, the dinosaurs had gone, and mammals, including the earliest horses, had begun to diversify and spread across the continent. Some 40 million years of erosion have mostly stripped these Mesozoic and early Cenozoic strata, nearly 6,000 feet thick, from the Grand Canyon region.

Surprisingly, the more recent part of Grand Canyon history, the cutting of the Canyon, is among the less well understood aspects of the story. On its journey to the sea the Colorado River flows across and through a variety of landscapes and structures. The headwaters of the Colorado River system rise in the Rocky Mountains of Colorado, Wyoming, and Utah. These mountains had their structural origin some 50 to 60 million years ago, well before the Colorado River system began. In mid-length the Colorado flows across the Colorado Plateau, where it has carved out major canyons. The eastern end of the Grand Canyon cuts through the Kaibab upwarp, a broadly

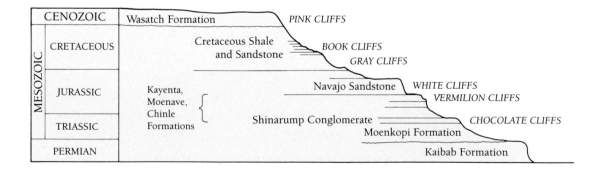

arched structure that was formed concurrently with the Rocky Mountains. At the mouth of the Grand Canyon the Colorado exits the Plateau through the Grand Wash Cliffs. On its way to the Gulf of California the river flows across fault structures and rocks of the Basin and Range Province that were produced by a great rifting, or pulling apart, within the last 17 million years.

There is compelling evidence from ancient river gravels that the upper part of the Colorado River system, in Colorado and Utah, was in existence as early as the early Miocene and possibly even the late Oligocene epochs (about 30 million years ago) and flowed towards Arizona. However, at the mouth of the Grand Canyon, immediately west of the Grand Wash Cliffs, the Colorado cuts through several thousand feet of more recent deposits of the late Miocene to early Pliocene, the youngest only about 6 million years old. These deposits consist of locally derived silt and sand plus limestone and other playa lake deposits that could only have formed in an interior undrained basin. No through-flowing Colorado River, and consequently no western Grand Canyon, could have existed here 6 million years ago. Yet evidence in southwestern Arizona clearly indicates that by about 5.3 million years ago the lower Colorado River emptied into an arm of the Gulf of California. Thus, the upper Colorado River system flowed southwest towards northern Arizona for 25 million years before the present lower Colorado could connect with it. Where did the ancestral upper Colorado River go?

One hypothesis suggests that the ancestral upper Colorado turned southeast from the present Marble Canyon in northern Arizona and flowed up the Little Colorado River drainage toward New Mexico and perhaps eventually into the Gulf of Mexico via the Rio Grande. After the Gulf of California opened, a southward- and westward-flowing drainage may have devel-

The Mesozoic staircase

oped in southern Arizona, extended across the southwestern
Colorado Plateau, and captured the upper Colorado system
near the present mouth of the Little Colorado River. After some
regional tilting of the land surface, the Little Colorado then
would have reversed itself and flowed from southeast to northwest. The lower and upper Colorado River systems would have
joined and then, as the Colorado Plateau was uplifted several
thousand feet, cut rapidly downward to produce the present
Grand Canyon.

However, more recently recognized evidence indicates that
the ancestral Colorado River never flowed southeast toward
New Mexico but instead may have crossed the Kaibab upwarp
in a shallow valley where the eastern Grand Canyon now exists.
A current hypothesis suggests that the river flowed northwest
toward Utah and central Nevada—the only direction not ruled
out by other evidence—perhaps eventually joining the Colum-
bia River system! After the opening of the Gulf of California the
northwest-flowing ancestral Colorado would have been captured west (rather than east) of the Kaibab upwarp by a newly
formed lower Colorado system draining to the gulf. Thus far,
no convincing evidence in southwestern Utah or central Nevada confirms that the ancestral Colorado ever went that way.

However the final connections were made, once the upper
and lower parts of the system were integrated, the Colorado
Plateau rose and the river kept pace by downcutting, carving
out the Grand Canyon. Clearly the Colorado River system has a
complex history: the present upper and lower parts of the system seem to have developed independently and separately until
integrated, in a manner not yet clearly understood, in the last
few million years.

A view of lava flows west from Toroweap. Lava Falls rapid is at the lower left

An equally dramatic and relatively recent chapter in Grand Canyon history reveals itself in volcanic activity in the central and western Grand Canyon. At Lava Falls, just above mile 180, the river drops thirty-seven feet as it pours over black lava boulders to form one of the biggest rapids in the Canyon. The lava boulders are stream-tumbled remnants of volcanic rocks that flowed down Toroweap Valley and into the Grand Canyon from the north. Layers of lava piled up nearly 2,000 feet deep in Toroweap Valley as they poured into the canyon. Additional lava cascaded over the inner canyon rim at Toroweap and downstream at Whitmore Wash (mile 187.5) and beyond.

Havasupai Indian fields

Still other lava flows were generated within the canyon, as evidenced by Vulcan's Forge, a small, cylindrical lava pinnacle that rises directly out of the river just upstream from Lava Falls and is the remnant of a volcanic neck that once occupied the throat of a volcano.

The accumulation of volcanic rocks in the central Canyon produced a huge lava dam many miles long and at least 1,500 feet high. Behind the dam a long, narrow lake must have formed as the water backed up through the Grand Canyon for some 200 miles, nearly to the foot of present-day Glen Canyon Dam. Recent detailed studies reveal that lava dams formed not once but four times at Toroweap. The oldest flows came about 1.2 million years ago, and the youngest about 350,000 years ago. Between major volcanic episodes the river re-excavated its canyon through the lava dams only to have the dams rebuilt by successive volcanic flows. Remnants of all four lava dams remain pasted high on the walls of the canyon below Vulcan's Throne at Toroweap and as patches of intracanyon flows near river level for many miles downstream.

In the upper Lake Mead area, the remnant of a lava flow 3.8 million years old directly overlies Colorado River gravels at Sandy Point in Iceberg Canyon—only 300 feet above the present canyon floor of the Colorado River. This indicates that at Iceberg Canyon the Colorado River had already cut down to within a few hundred feet of its present depth 3.8 million years ago.

The lowermost lava flow that enters the Canyon at Toroweap Valley is only 50 feet above the present river level, indicating that here the Colorado had excavated the Grand Canyon almost to its present depth by the time of the first lava dam, 1.2 million years ago. If the earliest date for a through-flowing river in the central and western Grand Canyon is accepted as about 5.5 million years ago, as previously discussed, then the Grand Canyon would have been carved out in 4.3 million years or less!

Four million years seems like a very short time in the framework of earth history. The river would have had to cut down 0.0012 feet per year or 1.2 feet per thousand years to form the Canyon—a remarkable but perhaps not unrealistic rate.

The volcanic record provides not only clues to the history of the Canyon but also an important site for rich farm land. At mile 157, thirty miles upstream from Toroweap Valley and the site of the lava dams, Havasu Creek enters the Grand Canyon from the south through Havasu Canyon. Eight miles upstream in Havasu Canyon is a shelf of limestone bedrock bearing topsoil, forming a peculiar flat 500-acre field perched halfway between the rim and the river. The Havasupai Indians have been farming that plot for the past seven hundred years, and other American Indians grew crops there even earlier.

That farmland, unique in the Canyon, occupies erosion-resistant limestone beds at the top of the Redwall Limestone and is at the same elevation as the presumed top of the highest lava dam at Toroweap. The Havasu farm appears to be the remains of the old delta formed by Havasu Creek when it dropped its load of sediment upon entering the lake formed behind the lava dam. But why was the delta not washed away when the dam was removed and the lake drained, as must have occurred elsewhere in the Canyon? Perhaps the unique circumstances of position atop the resistant Redwall Limestone and minimal erosion by Havasu Creek as it maintains its waterfalls and pools by extensive precipitation of travertine, have combined to preserve the Havasu farm as the only one of its kind in the Grand Canyon.

Within the last century, other human activities have begun to impinge on the Canyon and its history, particularly by dam building, which has changed forever the flow of water. The reservoirs behind the dams store water and also act as settling ponds into which drops most of the river-borne sediment. The erosive power of the river is locally diminished, and no doubt the rate of canyon cutting has decreased. Since the completion of Glen Canyon Dam in 1963, the beaches in the Grand Canyon—those slender and ephemeral ribbons of sand where thousands of river recreationists camp each year—have experienced major changes. Most appear to be gradually losing sand by the normal erosive effects of gravity, rainwash, flash floods, and fluctuating river flows. The pre-dam era having passed, the Colorado River now has little opportunity to replenish or maintain its beaches because of carefully controlled flows and the lack of periodic sediment-enriched spring floods.

The slow loss of beaches was interrupted in 1983 and 1984 when unexpectedly high, rapid runoff into an already filled Lake Powell required releases of water at a rate never experienced since the completion of Glen Canyon Dam. During two summers of these high water "spills," some of the beaches were completely removed but even more were rebuilt or newly constructed, so on balance there appears to have been more gain than loss of beach sand. Since then, however, the gradual depletion of the beaches has recommenced, with scant prospect that the river will replenish the sand as it did before the dam was built.

And so the history of the Grand Canyon continues. Despite, or perhaps in part because of, our imperfect understanding of it and our limited ability to manage the Canyon as a resource, it will surely remain throughout human history as one of the world's great places.

SUGGESTED READING

Baars, D. L., ed.

1969 *Geology and Natural History of the Grand Canyon Region.* Four Corners Geological Society, Fifth Annual Field Conference, Powell Centennial River Expedition, Durango, Colorado: The Society.

1983 *The Colorado Plateau: A Geologic History.* Albuquerque: University of New Mexico Press.

Beus, S. S., and M. Morales, eds.

1990 *Grand Canyon Geology.* Oxford: Oxford University Press.

Breed, W. J., and E. C. Roat, eds.

1974 *Geology of the Grand Canyon.* Flagstaff: Museum of Northern Arizona.

Collier, M.

1980 *An Introduction to Grand Canyon Geology.* Grand Canyon: Natural History Association.

Dutton, C. E.

1882 *Tertiary History of the Grand Canyon District* (with atlas). U.S. Geological Survey Monograph 2. Washington, D.C.: GPO. Reprint. Salt Lake City: Peregrine Smith, 1977.

Hunt, C. B.

1956 *Cenozoic History of the Colorado Plateau.* U.S. Geological Survey Professional Paper 279. Washington, D.C.: GPO.

Lucchitta, I.

1988 *Canyon Maker: A Geological History of the Colorado River.* Plateau 59 (2).

Powell, J. W.

1875 *Exploration of the Colorado River of the West and Its Tributaries.* Smithsonian Institution Annual Report. Reprint. New York: Dover Press, 1961.

Rabbitt, M. C., E. D. McKee, C. B. Hunt, and L. B. Leopold.

1969 *The Colorado River Region and John Wesley Powell.* U.S. Geological Survey Professional Paper 669. Washington, D.C.: GPO.

Stokes, W. L.

1973 *Scenes of the Plateau Lands and How They Came to Be.* Salt Lake City: Publishers Press.

2 / The Living Canyon

STEVEN W. CAROTHERS

The Grand Canyon is far more than a rock museum. Though dominated by spectacular rock forms, there are also within the Canyon biological communities unique unto themselves.

From any point on the rim of the Grand Canyon visitors can observe the lifeforms found on and beneath the canyon rims, a rewarding and informative experience. The interrelationships among temperature, moisture, vegetation, and animals can be read from the canyon environs in textbook detail.

The Colorado River and the separation of the canyon rims act as effective barriers to cross-canyon plant and animal dispersal. However, the Colorado River corridor at the canyon floor also serves as a pathway for the meeting of some species usually separated by hundreds of miles. An intensive search of canyon habitats reveals rare combinations of physical and biological features that have favored the existence of species found only in the Grand Canyon.

In modern times, as with most national parks, human visitors have had a profound impact on the biological features of the area. Sometimes the recent influences have destroyed habitats and species. In other cases the changes have created new habitats and added plant and animal species that were originally absent from the Canyon. Whether these changes are detrimental or beneficial overall is far too difficult for even seasoned naturalists to answer. This chapter merely hopes to provide an accounting of canyon life as it was and as it is now.

From the North Rim of the mile-deep chasm, with lush mountain meadows free from snow barely five months of the year, one can descend steeply by trail, in only a few hours, into a land of canyon deserts where snow and freezing temperatures are rare winter events. This climatological gradient of decreasing elevation and precipitation and increasing temperature has produced a continuum of biological habitat types that are usually found only by traversing hundreds of miles in latitude.

Plants and animals thrive within the confines of the Grand Canyon and the Colorado River. Over 400 vertebrate species are known to occupy the environs of Grand Canyon National Park (fishes, 26; amphibians, 6; reptiles, 35; mammals, 76; birds, 305). A few species, like the Grand Canyon rattlesnake, are found only in the Canyon. This docile reptile is unique in part for its salmon-colored skin, a characteristic that appears to be a protective adaptation to living on reddish or pink rocks. At least 1,500 different kinds of plants have been identified thus far, with over 800 of these species occurring along the 275-mile (Lees Ferry to Grand Wash Cliffs) streambank, or riparian corridor, of the river.

Dense coniferous forests mantle both the North and South rims at their highest elevations. Rising a thousand feet higher than the South Rim, the North Rim supports two distinct coniferous forest associations compared to only one on the South

Facing page 19: An aerial view downriver from the Unkar Delta

NORTH RIM

SOUTH RIM

SNOW
140 IN. (3,556 MM)

TEMPERATURE
MAX. AVER. JULY 84° F (31° C)
MIN. AVER. JAN. −8° F (−22° C)

ANNUAL PRECIPITATION
28 IN. (711 MM)

GROWING SEASON
141 DAYS

SNOW
61 IN. (1,549 MM)

TEMPERATURE
MAX. AVER. 93° F (34° C)
MIN. AVER. −1° F (−18° C)

ANNUAL PRECIPITATION
17 IN. (432 MM)

GROWING SEASON
96 DAYS

ASPEN-DOUGLAS FIR-
SPRUCE-PINE FOREST

PINYON-JUNIPER-SINGLE LEAF ASH WOODLAND

BLACKBRUSH-
MOJAVE DESERT

SNOW
6 IN. (152 MM)

ANNUAL PRECIPITATION
13 IN. (330 MM)

TEMPERATURE
MAX. AVER. 110° F (43° C)
MIN. AVER. 25° F (−4° C)

GROWING SEASON
275 DAYS

POST-DAM RIPARIAN

COLORADO
RIVER

8000'
KAIBAB
LIMESTONE
7000'
TOROWEAP LIMESTONE
COCONINO SANDSTONE
6000'
HERMIT SHALE
SUPAI FORMATION
5000'
REDWALL LIMESTONE
4000'
MUAV LIMESTONE AND DOLOMITE
BRIGHT ANGEL SHALE
3000'
TAPEATS SANDSTONE
PRECAMBRIAN
2000'

Grand Canyon vegetative zones

Rim. At its highest elevations, the North Rim produces a spruce-fir-aspen forest type interspersed with open mountain meadows nestled in shallow valleys. A dense cover of grasses and herbs carpet these meadows. Below the mixed conifer forest, the North Rim is covered by extensive stands of ponderosa pine, the same tree species that dominates the vegetation of the highest elevations of the South Rim. The most visible small animal populations of these high country areas are ground and tree squirrels, nuthatches, chickadees, juncos, and jays, while

A Grand Canyon rattlesnake (Photograph courtesy John Richardson)

eagles, deer, coyote, and an occasional mountain lion and bob-cat are the larger residents.

Below the rims, the conifers yield to the more evenly distributed but smaller pinyon and juniper trees. Shrubs, herbs, and grasses grow scattered throughout this woodland. Noisy extended families of pinyon jays and infrequent flocks of evening grosbeaks feast heavily on the pinyon nuts, a natural delicacy that was also an important source of food for early human inhabitants of the Canyon. This relatively imperfectly developed plant community extends downward for about 2,000 feet into the Canyon before meeting and mixing with the desert scrub plant association of the Tonto Platform.

Although the Tonto Platform of the interior canyon is only a few thousand feet below the rim's verdant forests, the intense summer heat and lack of moisture prevent any trees from growing except at the rare springs. Blackbrush, a low-growing shrub of the rose family, dominates the vegetation of the Tonto Platform, but Mormon tea, snakeweed, and numerous cacti are also common inhabitants. The most prominent animal in this area is the black-throated sparrow. Most of the small mammals have adopted a nocturnal lifestyle in their attempts to avoid the extremes of temperature and exposure.

In striking contrast to the surrounding desert, small seeps, springs, and perennial tributaries of the Inner Gorge support a luxuriant growth of water-loving vegetation. Common plants of these permanent water sources of the canyon backcountry include redbud, netleaf hackberry, willow and cottonwood trees, poison ivy, squawbush and similar woody shrubs, and an understory splashed with the colors of cardinal monkeyflower, columbine, maidenhair fern, rockmat, and many other surprises. The animals restricted to these specialized habitats are the dipper or water ouzel, the black phoebe, and the canyon tree frog.

Below the Tonto Platform, sparse scrub and cacti cling to the Inner Gorge cliffs, but the next substantial zone of vegetation occurs along the banks of the river. Prior to the placement of Glen Canyon and Hoover dams at either end of the Grand Canyon, the riparian habitats of the Colorado River endured periodic scouring floods, largely eradicated by the dams. A narrow band of mesquite, catclaw acacia, and Apache-plume marks an old preimpoundment high water line, while saltcedar, willow, arrowweed, and many other species proliferate in areas previously scoured by the uncontrolled river. Common birds and mammals of the riparian habitat are Lucy's warbler, Bell's vireo, blue grosbeak, beaver, and canyon, brush, and cactus mice.

A community of plants and animals is always changing, undergoing a continuous cycle of growth, reproduction, migration, and death. Members of a population, especially the young, commonly leave the area of their birth and attempt to reestablish in other suitable areas. This process of dispersal can be interrupted for some species when the dispersing plant or animal encounters geographic features such as high mountain ranges, deep canyons, impenetrable deserts, raging rivers, or other landforms that prohibit free passage. For other organisms, however, rivers running through deep canyons can actually serve as dispersal corridors; that is, a river and its associated habitat can act as a veritable highway for entry into areas that otherwise would be impenetrable.

Depending upon the organism, then, the Grand Canyon and its diversity of habitats function either as barriers to or corridors for dispersal. Hence, the Canyon becomes an important factor in determining the distribution patterns of local plants and animals. For the most part the Canyon is a barrier to rim-to-rim crossings and a corridor for passage along the length of the river or the Inner Gorge.

For example, scores of species of migratory waterfowl, shorebirds, and songbirds utilize the food and shelter provided by the Colorado River environs as they make their annual passage from breeding to wintering grounds. Sometimes these riverine habitats serve as the only suitable routes through otherwise barren and inhospitable regions.

Columbines along the river in the western Grand Canyon

The Colorado River corridor also provides a unique pathway for regional plant distribution. Though the desert of the interior canyon most closely resembles a typical Mohave Desert scene, species of the southern Sonoran and Chihuahuan deserts such as creosote bush, ocotillo, brittlebush, barrel cacti, and mortonia—as well as northern Great Basin Desert species like sagebrush and shadscale—live together as a single canyon flora. This unique combination results from the extreme depth and length of the Grand Canyon and its central geographic position in relation to the aforementioned deserts.

The occurrence and distribution of two closely related but distinctly different tree squirrels demonstrates one of the classical examples of the Canyon as a barrier to animal dispersal. To the south of the Grand Canyon and throughout suitable forested areas of Arizona and adjacent states, the grayish-colored Abert squirrel is common. Immediately north of the Canyon, in a relatively small (2,300-square-mile) area known as the Kaibab Plateau, the only known population of the black-and-white Kaibab squirrel is found. The common ancestor of these obviously related, but genetically distinct, animals once occupied a continuous distribution on both sides of the Colorado River, yet the two species became separated and isolated at some time in the recent geologic past.

Strong evidence indicates that 20,000 to 75,000 years ago (during the Wisconsin period of the Pleistocene), the climatic conditions around the Grand Canyon were significantly cooler and more moist. Forested rims characterized the ancient environment much as they do today; however, the additional moisture allowed the forests to extend much farther into the Canyon than at present. Although a river crossing would be a difficult and rare occasion for a squirrel-sized mammal, it could

Vaseys Paradise in Marble Canyon, from the rim

A desert bighorn sheep along the river

be accomplished by rafting on a fallen tree or even rock hopping during periods of low river flow. The important consideration here is that genetic interchange between the two rim populations took place during this colder period.

As the climate began to warm and the forests receded to the high country, the extensive deserts between the rims prevented the animals from traversing the Canyon, leaving the Kaibab population isolated on an island of forest in a sea of desert. In the time since their isolation, both populations of squirrels have undergone genetic changes that result in distinguishable morphological characteristics.

Although sufficient time and genetic change has not yet occurred for the Kaibab and Abert squirrels to be considered separate species (that is, it is likely that they can still interbreed
and produce viable offspring), their situation exemplifies the
evolutionary process in an early stage of the formation of distinct species from a common ancestor.

For some of the smaller Grand Canyon mammals, the river
can be an effective and apparently permanent blockade to free
movement. Two very similar but separate species of seed-eating
rodents occupy comparable habitats on opposite sides of the
river from southern Utah to the Gulf of California. The rock
pocket mouse lives on the south side of the river, while on the
north side lives the slightly larger long-tailed pocket mouse.
How the integrity of this distribution has survived accidental
rafting, low river flows, natural catastrophes, and time is enig-
matic; however, the Colorado River has clearly confined these
small mammals. For other animals, the natural influences may
be less apparent than the human.

The founding fathers of the National Park Service—John
Muir, Frederick Law Olmstead, and Stephen Mather—were
progressive conservationists of their day, principally interested
in protecting significant and beautiful natural resources from
human change. John Muir was one of the first naturalists to vo-
calize his fears that the pristine lands of the country would all
succumb to the pressures of economic exploitation. Muir was
driven, in his politically productive life, to save examples of our
natural heritage from the ravages of the plow and "hooved
locusts," Muir's term for domestic livestock.

Grand Canyon National Park was created in 1919, three
years after Congress passed the National Park Service Act, as
one of our first national parks. It is a popular misconception

that once an area is set aside as a national park, ecological changes either restore an area to its natural condition or are never allowed to occur in the first place. We like to believe that our park environments reflect a natural scenario of ecological succession uninfluenced by the human hand. As the scientific data accumulate, however, we become increasingly aware of how changes taking place both outside and within the boundaries of our parks damage these supposedly protected areas.

Additionally, management practices like predator control and fire suppression, once thought to be in harmony with a conservation ethic, are now known to have devastating influences on the dynamics of natural plant and animal communities. The terrible forest fires that ravaged more than a million acres of prime forest lands in Yellowstone National Park in 1988 resulted partly from fire management policies that had been implemented in the early part of this century. For many years, natural fires were suppressed quickly, so forest litter accumulated to a level that was beyond control once it began burning. Through time, without controlled burns (deliberately set forest fires designed to reduce the litter and deadwood fuel load), researchers expect that similar fires will destroy more forest lands.

The 1,915 square miles of Grand Canyon National Park are not free from the human imprint, nor will they ever be. Every park contains a resource management division of naturalists, scientists, and managers dedicated to assessing the ecological status of the land and when possible, restoring or mitigating damage. The Grand Canyon has a very strong and active management program primarily involved with the challenge of protecting the park environments from the impact of more than three million visitors a year.

Park managers continually encounter political and economic forces pressuring for the expansion of visitor facilities or commercial uses of the backcountry, air space, and river corridor. The more insidious threats, however, do not result from direct use of the park but from activities initiated outside the park. For example, Grand Canyon air quality is influenced from pollutants produced as far away as the Los Angeles Basin. Recent studies have further emphasized the environmental effects on the Colorado River of its two major dams, Hoover and Glen Canyon. Both are placed several miles outside the park, one at either end of the Canyon; both result in major changes to the aquatic, terrestrial, and physical resources of the canyon interior.

The resource managers have won some victories. During the late 1970s, a controversial plan to eliminate feral (wild) burros from the Canyon met with substantial opposition from an uninformed public. These descendants of previously domesticated burros once utilized by prospectors throughout the Canyon were growing in numbers, overgrazing and otherwise damaging park resources. Yet in the public mind the burros belonged in the Grand Canyon, and people emotionally and politically resisted the elimination plan. After park managers educated the public to the unnaturalness of the burro in the Grand Canyon and to the severe damage these animals caused the other resources, more than five hundred burros were airlifted from the Canyon. Today, the burro has been eliminated from the fauna of the area and probably never will be reintroduced. As a result, the previously damaged habitats are healing. Other human changes are not so easily solved.

When Hoover Dam was officially opened in 1935 and Lake Mead began to fill, portions of the Colorado River in the Grand

Canyon were destined to change from a riverine to a lacustrine (lake) environment. The changes in the river's channel caused by Lake Mead affect streambank ecology for thirty miles upstream from the westernmost boundary of the Canyon at the Grand Wash Cliffs.

The lake also acts as a dispersal center for non-native fish species such as striped bass, green sunfish, carp, and a variety of minnows. These "unnatural" elements of the lake fishery have invaded the upper reaches of the Grand Canyon. Scientists do not fully understand the biological consequences of exotic lake fishes, as well as other aquatic organisms invading the riverine environment; however, they do know that exotic species can often detrimentally influence native species.

The impacts of Lake Mead on the riverine ecology of the Grand Canyon are almost inconsequential when compared to the changes brought about by the 710-foot-high Glen Canyon Dam. Officially operational in 1963 and located seventeen miles upstream from the park boundary, Glen Canyon Dam has completely altered the Colorado River within the park. The dam has changed the physical and biological characteristics of the river while simultaneously enhancing river recreation activities.

Today, the demand for hydroelectric power controls the river's flow. When distant cities need more power, more water is released from the penstocks of Glen Canyon Dam. Because the water is released from two hundred feet below the lake's surface (the hypolimnion), it is perpetually cold and virtually sediment-free. River temperatures in the Grand Canyon now range from 45 to 55°F (7 to 13°C) where they once approached 80°F (27°C). The sediment entering Lake Mead has been reduced to less than 15 percent of the total pre-dam sediment volume. The water's flow rarely exceeds 28,000 cubic feet per second (cfs) now and averages a mere 10,000 cfs.

The difference in sediment concentration and water temperature have had a profound impact on the aquatic ecosystem. The clear, cold water now released from the dam has changed the river's productivity from low to high. Solar radiation previously reflected from the surface of muddy water now penetrates to the bottom of the river, allowing abundant production of algae and associated periphyton. This new productivity is the basis for a food chain that supports a trout fishery recognized as one of the best in existence.

Unfortunately, the once-common native fishes of the pre-dam regimen have nearly disappeared. Of the original eight native fish species known to have occurred within the Canyon during historic times, three (the Colorado squawfish and the roundtail and bonytail chubs) are no longer present; one (the razorback sucker) is so infrequently found that, for all practical purposes, it has been extirpated from the system; and another (the humpback chub, a federally listed endangered species) is limited in distribution to only a tiny portion of its former range. The three remaining native species (the flannelmouth and bluehead suckers and the speckled dace) now share the aquatic habitats of the Grand Canyon with many other introduced species. The most common fish of the Colorado River in the Grand Canyon today is the rainbow trout.

Although Glen Canyon Dam has been responsible for altering the aquatic habitat, the change from a native, endemic fishery to a primarily exotic fishery began long before the dam's construction. The most significant impact on the fishery prior to the dam was the introduction of carp and channel catfish in the late part of the 1800s. The catfish efficiently prey on the

young of the native species, while the carp can displace the indigenous fish from habitats and compete for the limited food resources.

From 1963, when Glen Canyon Dam began storing Colorado River water in Lake Powell, until 1983, the highest flow in the Canyon was about 50,000 cfs, and that only for a portion of a day while the spillways were tested. By reducing the annual peak flow from 86,000 cfs to 28,000 cfs, the dam made significant changes in stream bank characteristics. Before the dam controlled the river channel, any plants downslope of the high water line had been annuals, usually having at most only one year to grow between floods. But for twenty years after completion of the dam, a pattern of stabilized flows existed, and a new band of riparian vegetation appeared in the old scour zone.

Once the lake filled in 1980, though, it was only a matter of time before a high snowpack in the Rocky Mountains, a wet spring and summer, and a full lake would combine—requiring exceptionally high releases from Glen Canyon Dam. In June of 1983 the floods returned to the Grand Canyon; flows reached almost 100,000 cfs for nearly a week, but unusually high flows of 45,000 to 60,000 cfs lasted for months. The river scoured the bank as it had been in the past and removed almost 40 percent of the "new" riparian vegetation.

The uniqueness of the new high-water-line riparian vegetation and the human-influenced conditions under which it was originally allowed to proliferate provide a classic ecological story. The new zone of vegetation consists primarily of the nonnative salt cedar or tamarisk tree, but coyote willow, seepwillow, desert broom, and arrowweed are also fairly common components. Moreover, evidence indicates that the plants of the pre-dam high-water-line community—mesquites, acacias,

Tapeats Creek

and a scattering of hackberry trees—are moving downslope to colonize the new zone. Contrary to classical wildlife management wisdom, the non-native tamarisk tree provides substantial habitat for native species of birds, reptiles, and small mammals. The tamarisk and other plants in the new high-water zone vegetation have become vital habitat, changing the density and distribution of native riparian animals in the Grand Canyon.

In the absence of summer peak discharges of water laden with sediment, slowly but steadily the total beach surface is being eroded and cut back. Though some of these beaches have become partially stabilized with the new riparian habitat, the water release patterns from the dam and the constant threat of additional floods leave the future of the beaches and vegetation somewhat uncertain. Numerous researchers are studying the ultimate fate of the streambanks and the terrestrial wildlife and vegetation living thereon. The Bureau of Reclamation, the National Park Service, and the Arizona Game and Fish Department are participating in what is known as the Glen Canyon Environmental Studies, a multiyear interdisciplinary investigation designed to evaluate dam-related impacts to the riverine environment in the Canyon.

Concomitant with the dam-related changes in the natural riverine environment, park managers have seen a dramatic increase in the number of white-water recreationists "running" the Colorado. In 1967, barely 2,100 people chartered passage on the river. By the end of 1973, 15,000 people per year were enjoying this experience, an increase in use of about 700 percent in six years. Much of the increase in use can be attributed to the control of the river by Glen Canyon Dam. Reasonably predictable water releases now allow precise trip scheduling, and the hazards of navigating the river during peak flood dis-

A redbud tree in Deer Creek narrows

charge rarely occur. This increased human activity in the Canyon has damaged beach and backcountry environments. Most river outfitters, however, observe extreme caution, and the policies and procedures the National Park Service has developed for conscientious river running have resulted in minimal impact on the entire system.

As world population pressures continue to increase, consumptive demands on the natural resource base will inevitably further threaten environments that have not yet been completely altered by the exhaustive foraging of the human species. The large expanses of near-pristine landscapes administered by the National Park Service have thus far been protected from total resource utilization. Yet every year we have more and more park visitors, and though their demands are largely nonconsumptive in nature, the resource can often be irreparably damaged by merely providing the masses access to these pristine areas. Additionally, the insidious web of environmental pollution and manipulation originating outside our national parks increasingly spreads its disruption throughout these areas we attempt to protect.

Portions of the Grand Canyon and the Colorado River within the national park have undergone significant changes as a direct result of recreational use and the impact of modern technological advances. As the river has changed, so also has the distribution and density of the native lifeforms that evolved under the natural river regimen. Some of these changes are regrettable, and some are not. Native species have become endangered, while exotic or introduced species have proliferated, often at the expense of the native flora and fauna. However, the new zone of vegetation within the riparian corridor has clearly enhanced the density and distribution of many native terrestrial wildlife forms.

Along and within the river, we now have a naturalized community of plants and animals that could reach a point of stability if future floods from Glen Canyon Dam are managed appropriately. The environmental studies underway in the Canyon have that management scenario as their goal.

Though certain human-related changes have affected portions of the natural resource base in the Grand Canyon, the vast majority of this 1,227,850-acre national park remains in a pristine state. The ongoing scientific research on the basic elements of the Canyon's biotic communities and the park managers' continued searches for damage to those resources are the only insurance we can offer future generations for whom the parks have ultimately been set aside.

Neither the industrial world nor wilderness users can ignore the fragility of the Grand Canyon ecosystem. It is crucial that the visitor to the Grand Canyon, whether car-camper, back-packer, or white-water enthusiast, be educated concerning the ecology and ecological problems of the area and that he or she be aware of how to minimize the human impact on the Canyon and its wildlife.

The Grand Canyon is an incredible landform containing plant and animal associations found nowhere else. To recognize the Canyon's uniqueness is to be inspired with the necessity of its preservation.

SUGGESTED READING

Aitchison, S. W.
 1977 The Grand Canyon is a world in itself. *Plateau* 49(4): 3–9.

Brown, B. T., et al.
 1978 *Birds of the Grand Canyon Region: An Annotated Checklist.* Grand Canyon Natural History Association, Monograph 1. Grand Canyon: Natural History Association.

Brown, B. T., S. W. Carothers, and R. Johnson
 1987 *Grand Canyon Birds: Historical Notes, Natural History, and Ecology.* Tucson: University of Arizona Press.

Carothers, S. W.
 1977 Man's use of the Grand Canyon: is it time for a change? *Plateau* 49(4):24–31.

Carothers, S. W., and S. W. Aitchison, eds.
 1976 *An Ecological Survey of the Riparian Zone of the Colorado River between Lees Ferry and the Grand Wash Cliffs, Arizona.* Final report submitted to the National Park Service.

Carothers, S. W., and B. T. Brown
 1991 *The Colorado River Through Grand Canyon: Natural History and Human Change.* Tucson: University of Arizona Press.

Hoffmeister, D. F.
 1971 *Mammals of Grand Canyon.* Urbana: University of Illinois Press.

Lowe, C. H.
 1964 *The Vertebrates of Arizona.* Tucson: University of Arizona Press.

McDougall, W. B.
 1964 *Grand Canyon Wild Flowers.* Flagstaff and Grand Canyon: Museum of Northern Arizona and Natural History Association.

Phillips, A. M., III.
 1977 A botanist's view. *Plateau* 49(4):10–17.

1979   *Grand Canyon Wildflowers: A Photographic Essay.* Grand
       Canyon: Natural History Association.
Reichman, O. J., and G. Ruffner
    1977   Life in a narrow world: Grand Canyon ecology. *Plateau*
           49(4):18–23.
United States Department of the Interior
    1988   *Glen Canyon Environmental Studies Final Report.* Salt Lake
           City: U.S. Bureau of Reclamation.

3 / Grand Canyon Indians

ROBERT C. EULER

Never underestimate the importance of an artifact, even one made of so humble a parentage as the willow tree. If it were not for split-willow figurines found in the Grand Canyon in 1933, and later companion findings, we might not know that human beings visited the canyon floor some 2,000 years before Christ was born. Though we don't know much more than that about these prehistoric American Indians—there's a limit to how much we can read from a willow twig wound around itself—we can say with reasonable certainty that they were familiar with the depths of the Grand Canyon almost 4,000 years before John Wesley Powell floated the first scientific expedition down the Colorado River.

They were hunters and gatherers, these American Indians, and lived in what archaeologists call an Archaic period. This much we can safely surmise. They came from the Desert West. They deposited their artfully constructed split-willow animal figures in limestone caves, probably as a form of imitative magic ritually depicting the animals they wished to hunt. Indeed, recently, archaeologists located an almost-inaccessible cave in the Canyon that contained figurines surrounded by cairns of rock—probably a shrine.

A few years ago, in excavations at prehistoric sites along the Colorado River, archaeologist Anne Trinkle Jones of the National Park Service uncovered campsites of people who lived in the Canyon somewhat later than those who made the figurines. The Archaic levels of these shelters date from between 1135 and 85 B.C. These people probably lived in those shallow caves and hunted deer, bighorn sheep, and other animals with spears. At certain seasons they also gathered edible wild plants. Domestic crops were probably unknown to them, as were the bow and arrow.

Researchers also recently discovered an Archaic site apparently unique to the Grand Canyon. This is a series of pictographs—paintings on the rock wall of a cave—probably related to similar examples of a religious nature farther north, in Utah. While archaeologists have not precisely dated this site, the style of painting indicates it was done sometime between 2000 B.C. and A.D. 1.

These newly discovered Archaic sites, together with the split-twig figurines such as those found in Stanton's Cave in Marble Canyon and the earlier discovery of Archaic Pinto-style spear points on Red Butte, near the South Rim of the Canyon, certainly point to a rather widespread use of the gorge by American Indians before the time of Christ. It is not presently possible to relate these people to any of the later occupants of the Grand Canyon, at least not with any degree of reliability. They disappeared into the mists of prehistory. Where they went and why, we do not know.

But all the same, these early people contributed immeasurably to our knowledge of the Grand Canyon. Because they left

Facing page 43: Anasazi granaries in the cliffs at Nankoweap Creek

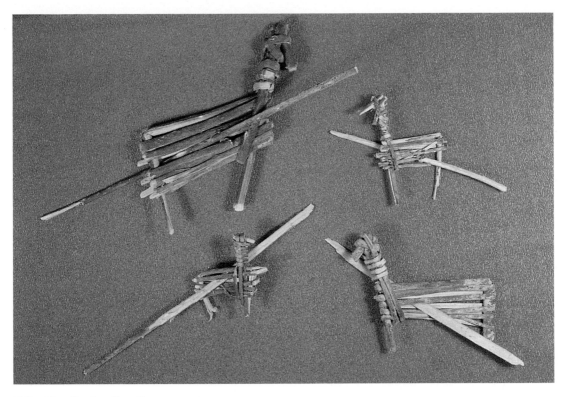

Split-willow figurines from Stanton's Cave

those small artifacts and paintings, we know they existed, and it makes a difference of some 2,500 years in our chronicling of human use of the Canyon as living environment. Before the figurines were found, archaeologists had dated the first habitation of the Canyon to about A.D. 500 with the advent of the Anasazi or Pueblo Indians, a people much more culturally advanced than their Archaic precursors.

The Anasazi, thought to be direct ancestors of the present-day Hopi of northern Arizona, probably began as a Desert Culture people in the Great Basin. Sometime around the year A.D. 1 or slightly earlier, they moved into the northern portion of

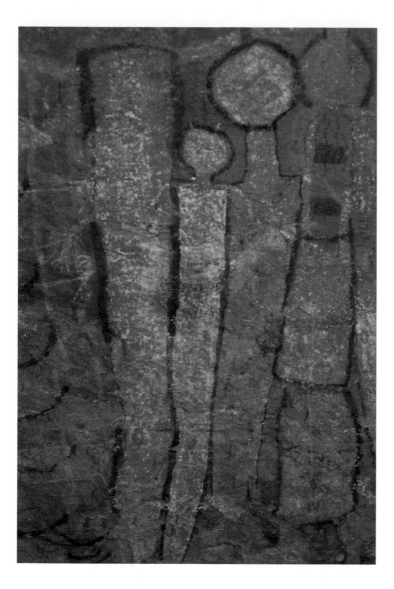

Archaic pictographs from the western Grand Canyon (Photograph by Frank Tikalsky)

the Southwest. Archaeologists refer to this period in their culture as that of the "Basketmaker," for rather obvious reasons. Using rudimentary techniques, these hunters and gatherers added corn and squash to their agricultural capability and hunted deer, bighorn sheep, and rabbits.

The Basketmaker style of life changed in several ways around A.D. 500. They developed new varieties of corn and planted beans. By grouping circular pit houses they began village life. They manufactured fired pottery and supplemented spear-throwing with the use of the bow and arrow to kill game.

This stable economic base, combining hunting and gathering with the beginnings of diversification of crops, allowed the Anasazi to intensify and expand their territory and cultural achievements. After learning to grow cotton, they added spinning and loom weaving to their repertory, weaving fabric clothing and adding objects of personal adornment. They learned to make exquisite pottery. Thus, midway through the eleventh century A.D., Pueblo culture flowered into its classic traditions. This period, continuing into historic times, saw the rise of great communal pueblos, up to five stories high; these high-rise apartment dwellings housed several hundred people, and community living must have become highly organized. Evidence indicates that authority centered on a theocratic hierarchy of priests.

The Anasazi of the Grand Canyon lived on the fringe of this great cultural florescence. Some evidence indicates that they made sporadic forays into the Canyon beginning about A.D. 500 or slightly earlier. By the middle of the eleventh century, however, they apparently found climatic conditions there to their liking, and between about A.D. 1050 and 1150, hundreds of sites were occupied in myriad recesses of the Canyon and on both the North and South rims.

These were mostly small, one-to-ten-room surface masonry houses with associated storage rooms, agave roasting pits, and occasional subterranean religious structures—kivas—in front of the pueblo. While we know the Anasazi grew domestic crops near their dwellings, new evidence from a small village occupied between A.D. 1049 and 1064 in the Coconino Basin near the South Rim suggests that corn, beans, and squash were not all-important in the Anasazi diet. This village had burned catastrophically, and normally perishable foods had turned to charcoal and were preserved. The evidence from this site indicates that its inhabitants focused on the exploitation and use of pinyon nuts and other wild seeds rather than on farming.

About the time the Anasazi were beginning to explore the Grand Canyon, the Cohonina, another group of American Indians from west-central Arizona, were settling along the South Rim and in Havasu Canyon. The Cohonina achieved a veneer of Pueblo culture by imitating the pottery of the Anasazi and attempting to build similar masonry houses. They farmed essentially the same crops and of course hunted the same game, though to a lesser extent. Their social and religious life probably differed considerably from that of the Anasazi.

Some time about A.D. 1150, both the Anasazi and the Cohonina abandoned their settlements in and around the Grand Canyon. Though the Cohonina disappeared from the archaeological record, the Anasazi consolidated their numbers along more reliable watercourses—the Little Colorado, Rio Grande, and (usually) infallible springs of the Hopi country. For more than a century and a half the Canyon remained completely uninhabited by human beings.

*An Anasazi pottery cache off the
North Rim*

Then, about A.D. 1300, the Cerbat people, direct ancestors of
the Walapai and Havasupai, moved from the southern deserts
near the lower Colorado River to the high plateaus that had
been the Cohonina and Anasazi homeland south of the Grand
Canyon. The Cerbat lived in rock shelters and impermanent
brush wickiups. Though hunting and gathering were their economic mainstay, they were incipient farmers who planted their
crops near permanent springs. Although their material culture
was simple, they established a stable way of life on the plateau,
for they remained there until the 1880s, when the U.S. Army
forcibly removed them to their present reservations.

An Anasazi ruin below the South Rim

At nearly the same time as the Cerbat, another seminomadic people approached the Grand Canyon from the northwest horizon. Ancestors of the Southern Paiute, they settled along the North Rim of the Canyon and carried on an existence not too different from their South Rim neighbors, the Cerbat. They, too, remained in this aboriginal territory until Anglo-Americans established reservations for them in the late nineteenth century.

It was these native peoples—the Pueblos, Cohonina, Havasupai, Walapai, and the Southern Paiute—who form the indigenous history of the Grand Canyon. Present-day visitors to the Grand Canyon may wonder how these early people could have survived the harsh summer environment of the canyon depths—and why they chose to try in the first place. Spectacular though the Canyon is, they did not live there for aesthetic reasons. The choice was a matter of survival, and they survived because they adapted their culture to fit their natural environment.

Pueblo occupation of the Canyon was apparently in large part seasonal due to the varying nature of food supplies from the Inner Gorge to the rims and to the warmer winter climate in the lower elevations. In the summer, many people moved to the rims to farm. Indeed, one of the most significant agricultural communities of the twelfth-century Anasazi was located on the plateau near the Canyon's rim, where, in addition to farming, deer hunting and an abundance of edible wild plants contributed to their well-balanced economy.

Vegetal foods available to the prehistoric inhabitants of the Grand Canyon. Left to right: yucca fruits, pinyon nuts, prickly-pear fruits.

But below the rims, they also hunted bighorn sheep and rabbits. Below the rims they could feast on the fruits of cactus, the
beans of the mesquite, and the tender crowns of the agave
plant. More important, at 3,000 feet below the rims, they found
long, almost frost-free growing seasons for their gardens. Sufficient water supply made it possible for them to farm in the recesses of side canyons where they discovered many springs.

Throughout many of these tributary canyons as well as on
the rims, especially in the eastern portion of the Grand Canyon,
we find Pueblo masonry ruins in association with low, agricultural check dams—abundant evidence that these farmers prac-
ticed erosional control and other conservation methods. There
is a strong correlation between location of prehistoric habitation sites and access routes into the Canyon where its sheer
walls have broken down, clear indications that the inhabitants
moved with relative ease from rim to rim and throughout the
Canyon. Archaeologists now know more than one hundred
routes used by canyon dwellers to gain access.

Environmentally, then, the Canyon provided excellent resources to sustain Pueblo life, and they apparently made intelligent use of those resources. So why did they and their
Cohonina neighbors leave the Canyon?

Archaeologists once believed that their disappearance coin-
cided with the advent of the Cerbat on plateaus along the
South Rim and the coming of the forerunners of the Southern
Paiute to the high, forested lands near the North Rim. Now evidence indicates that, at least in the Grand Canyon, the
pre-1150 and post-1300 residents missed each other by more
than a century. Certainly nothing indicates that the Cerbat, the
ancestors of the Pai (as the combined Walapai and Havasupai
once termed themselves), or the Southern Paiute forced the
Anasazi and Cohonina abandonment.

Recently, teams of scientists including archaeologists, botanists, and geologists have made detailed studies of past climates around the Grand Canyon. Early in the twelfth century, there were many years of increasingly severe drought. By A.D. 1150, most of the Cohonina and Anasazi farmers could no longer cope with these deteriorating environmental conditions in an agriculturally marginal area; thus, they abandoned the Canyon for more favorable climes.

When conditions improved in the fourteenth century, the Pai spread over the southern plateau and penetrated much of the western and central part of the Canyon. They soon reached their maximum range and occupied all of the southern portion of the Grand Canyon and its plateau east to the Little Colorado River. Here they hunted, gathered, and farmed near permanent streams and springs. The habitation sites discovered within the Canyon consist of rock shelters having floors strewn with cultural debris including reddish-brown potsherds, flat slab milling stones, and arrow points, all differing from those of the Cohonina or the Anasazi.

The Southern Paiute maintained a similar existence on the North Rim uplands and in their tributary canyons from the fourteenth century on. Their finger-incised brown pottery, milling stones, and arrow points differed somewhat from those of the Pai, but they also occupied rock shelters and roasted agave in stone-ringed pits. That they sometimes camped in abandoned Pueblo ruins is evident from discovery of their pottery mixed with that of the Anasazi around masonry structures.

Both the Pai and the Paiute cultures were stable and long-lived. From about 1300 until the latter part of the nineteenth century they continued to use the natural resources of the Grand Canyon. Both groups maintained amicable trade relations with the Puebloans in the present Hopi country, as evi-

A Havasupai village scene

denced by fragments of Pueblo ceramics found on many
Havasupai, Walapai, and Southern Paiute ruins in the Grand
Canyon. This yellow pottery, exquisitely decorated with designs
in brownish-black paint similar to the Hopi ceramics of today,
was probably traded to the Hopi for deer skins, red paint, and
agave. From 1300 to relatively recently, the Hopi seem to have
periodically returned to ceremoniously collect salt from a natural deposit near the confluence of the Little Colorado and Colorado rivers.

Though archaeologists need to learn much more, our exist-
ing data suggest a fairly coherent history of canyon habitation

for more than four thousand years. Because of the rich legacy of artifacts left us by the Anasazi and, to a lesser degree, by the Cohonina, Pai, and Paiute, we can deduce what they were like and can envision somewhat their lifestyles. The same is not true of the Canyon's original inhabitants, the split-willow artists and other Archaic peoples who sat in those limestone caves so long ago.

But why be pessimistic? The willow-twig artifacts waited more than 3,000 years to be discovered and then had to wait another decade before radiocarbon dating established their age. And some of these twig animals were found still standing upright in the dust of canyon caves.

Never underestimate the patience of an artifact!

SUGGESTED READING: ARCHAEOLOGY

For general background:

Cordell, L. S.
 1984   *Prehistory of the Southwest.* New York: Academic Press.

For specific Grand Canyon references:

Emslie, S. D., R. C. Euler, and J. I. Mead
 1987   A desert culture shrine in Grand Canyon, Arizona, and the role of split-twig figurines. *National Geographic Research* 3(4):511–16.

Euler, R. C.
 1967   The canyon dwellers. *American West* 4(2):22–29.
 1984   *The Archaeology, Geology, and Paleobiology of Stanton's Cave, Grand Canyon National Park, Arizona.* Grand Canyon Natural History Association, Monograph 6. Grand Canyon: Natural History Association.

Fowler, D. D., R. C. Euler, and C. S. Fowler
 1969   *John Wesley Powell and the Anthropology of the Canyon Country.* U.S. Geological Survey Professional Paper 670. Washington, D.C.: GPO.

Jones, A. T.
 1986   *A Cross Section of Grand Canyon Archaeology: Excavations at Five Sites Along the Colorado River.* Western Archaeological and Conservation Center, Publications in Anthropology 28. Tucson: National Park Service.

Jones, A. T., and R. C. Euler
 1979   *A Sketch of Grand Canyon Prehistory.* Grand Canyon: Natural History Association.

Schwartz, D. W., M. P. Marshall, and J. Kepp
 1979   *Archaeology of the Grand Canyon: The Bright Angel Site.* Santa Fe: School of American Research Press.

Schwartz, D. W., R. C. Chapman, and J. Kepp
 1980   *Archaeology of the Grand Canyon: Unkar Delta.* Santa Fe: School of American Research Press.

Schwartz, D. W., J. Kepp, and R. C. Chapman
 1981   *Archaeology of the Grand Canyon: The Walhalla Plateau.* Santa Fe: School of American Research Press.

Sullivan, A. P., III

1986 *Prehistory of the Upper Basin, Coconino County, Arizona.* Archaeological Series 167, Cultural Resource Management Division. Tucson: Arizona State Museum, University of Arizona.

SUGGESTED READING: ETHNOLOGY

For general background:

Dutton, B. P.

1975 *Indians of the American Southwest.* Albuquerque: University of New Mexico Press.

For specific reference to American Indians around the Grand Canyon:

PAI

Cushing, F. H.

1965 *The Nation of the Willows.* Flagstaff: Northland Press (reprint of 1882 original).

Dobyns, H. F., and R. C. Euler

1967 *The Ghost Dance of 1889 Among the Pai Indians of Northwestern Arizona.* Prescott: Prescott College Press.

1970 *Wauba Yuma's People: The Comparative Socio-Political Structure of the Pai Indians of Northwestern Arizona.* Prescott: Prescott College Press.

1971 *The Havasupai People.* Phoenix: Indian Tribal Series.

1976 *The Walapai People.* Phoenix: Indian Tribal Series.

Hirst, S.

1985 *Havsuw 'Baaja: People of the Blue Green Water.* Supai, Arizona: Havasupai Tribe.

McKee, B., E. McKee, and J. Herold

1975 *Havasupai Baskets and Their Makers: 1930–1940.* Flagstaff: Northland Press.

Smithson, C. L.

1959 *The Havasupai Woman.* University of Utah Anthropological Papers 38. Salt Lake City: University of Utah.

Smithson, C. L., and R. C. Euler
  1964 *Havasupai Religion and Mythology.* University of Utah Anthropological Papers 68. Salt Lake City: University of Utah.
Spier, L.
  1928 *Havasupai Ethnography.* New York: American Museum of Natural History.
Weber, S. A., and P. D. Seaman, eds.
  1985 *Havasupai Habitat.* Tucson: University of Arizona Press.

HOPI

Euler, R. C., and H. F. Dobyns
  1971 *The Hopi People.* Phoenix: Indian Tribal Series.
Page, S., and J. Page
  1986 *Hopi.* New York: Harry N. Abrams, Inc.
Thompson, L.
  1950 *Culture in Crisis: A Study of the Hopi Indians.* New York: Harper & Brothers.
Titiev, M.
  1944 *Old Oraibi: A Study of the Hopi Indians of Third Mesa.* Cambridge: Peabody Museum of Harvard.
Wright, B.
  1977 *Hopi Kachinas.* Flagstaff: Northland Press.
Wright, M.
  1972 *Hopi Silver.* Flagstaff: Northland Press.

NAVAJO

Bailey, G., and R. Bailey
  1986 *A History of the Navajos.* Santa Fe: School of American Research Press.
Bighorse, T.
  1990 *Bighorse The Warrior.* Tucson: University of Arizona Press.
Dedera, D.
  1975 *Navajo Rugs.* Flagstaff: Northland Press.
Dobyns, H. F., and R. C. Euler
  1977 *The Navajo Indians.* Phoenix: Indian Tribal Series.

Kluckhohn, C., and D. C. Leighton
1951 *The Navaho.* Cambridge: Harvard University Press.
Leighton, A. H., and D. C. Leighton
1945 *The Navaho Door.* Cambridge: Harvard University Press.
Leighton, D. C., and C. Kluckhohn
1948 *Children of the People.* Cambridge: Harvard University Press.
Woodward, A.
1971 *Navajo Silver.* Flagstaff: Northland Press.

SOUTHERN PAIUTE

Anonymous
1976 *Nuwuvi: A Southern Paiute History.* Inter-Tribal Council of Nevada. Salt Lake City: University of Utah Printing Service.
Bunte, P. A., and R. J. Franklin
1987 *From the Sands to the Mountain: Change and Persistence in a Southern Paiute Community.* Lincoln: University of Nebraska Press.
Euler, Robert C.
1972 *The Paiute People.* Phoenix: Indian Tribal Series.

4 / *Historical Explorations*

ROBERT C. EULER

While the credit for all early exploration of the Grand Canyon must be given to American Indians, they of course left no written record of their exploits. The first documentary accounts of the Grand Canyon were penned by the earliest Europeans to visit the region in the year 1540.

The explorer Francisco Vásquez de Coronado had ridden from Mexico at the head of a great entourage of Spaniards and Indians. In the summer of 1540, while at the New Mexico pueblo of Zuni, he heard about the Hopi to the west and dispatched one of his lieutenants, Pedro de Tovar, to investigate. Tovar was the first white man to visit the Hopi, and he returned to tell Coronado about a great river the Hopi had told him lay farther west. Coronado sent another of his officers, García López de Cárdenas, back to Hopi where he procured guides. According to the official chronicler for the Coronado expedition, Cárdenas journeyed twenty days westerly from the Hopi towns before seeing the Grand Canyon, thus becoming the first European to do so. We don't know exactly where the Spaniards were, but probably they arrived at the Canyon's rim somewhere in the vicinity of Desert View. They spent the better part of three days trying to descend into the Canyon, which they noted was three to four leagues (eight to ten miles) wide. After getting no more than a third of the way down, they gave up. Interestingly, their Hopi guides, undoubtedly familiar with the trails into the gorge, refrained from revealing their locations to Cárdenas.

These sixteenth-century Spaniards were interested only in gold (to bolster a sagging economy at home) and in converts to Christianity. Finding neither at the Grand Canyon, the small expedition returned to Coronado and the main party at Zuni.

If our historical records are accurate, Europeans did not again visit the Canyon until 1776. While Americans along the eastern seaboard prepared to declare their independence from Great Britain, two Spanish expeditions, both with different purposes, were abroad in the Grand Canyon country. In the summer of that year, the Franciscan missionary Francisco Tomás Garcés traveled by mule from southern Arizona to the missions in California and then back into northern Arizona. He heard about the Walapai and Havasupai and on an intended journey to Zuni decided to visit them. Alone except for some Hopi guides, Garcés spent a number of days journeying through the country of the Walapai and then became the first European of record to visit the Havasupai in their Grand Canyon home. From Supai he rode along the South Rim of the Canyon to the Hopi towns, where he arrived on July 4, 1776. Meeting an unfriendly reception there, he retraced his entire route back into Havasu Canyon and returned to his mission of San Xavier del Bac near Tucson late in the summer.

In that same year, two other Franciscan priests, Silvestre Vélez de Escalante and Francisco Atanasio Domínguez, with a

Facing page 61: The Havasupai village deep in the Grand Canyon

small escort of soldiers, rode north from Santa Fe searching for an easy route to California. At Utah Lake south of Salt Lake City, with winter approaching, they decided to turn south and entered the Grand Canyon region along the Arizona-Utah border in the territory of the Southern Paiute. Warned of the impassability of the Canyon, the party turned east without having seen its rims. They crossed the Colorado River at a ford now submerged beneath the waters behind Glen Canyon Dam and returned to Santa Fe by way of the Hopi villages.

This was the end of Spanish exploration of the Grand Canyon area. Their ventures in North America concluded in 1821 when Mexico achieved its independence, and the Mexicans had concerns closer to home than the Grand Canyon.

The Grand Canyon region became part of the United States after the Mexican War of 1848, but Anglo-American fur trappers had already passed through the area. Most of these—Kit Carson, Jedediah Smith, Antoine Leroux, and Bill Williams, to name some—left few records. However, in 1826, James Ohio Pattie claimed to have traveled along or near the South Rim of the Canyon after hunting for beaver along the lower Colorado River. Pattie's journal is replete with exaggerations, however, and there is no compelling evidence that he actually saw the great gorge.

After the United States acquired the vast southwestern region, the government sent numerous official expeditions to the territory. In 1851, Captain Lorenzo Sitgreaves was ordered to determine the navigability of the Zuni and Little Colorado rivers. Descending down the latter stream to Black Falls, east of the Grand Canyon, he finally decided that the often-dry river could not be navigated by boat and turned west, missing the Grand Canyon by a number of miles. Sitgreaves was followed

Sus-quat-a-mi, war chief of the Walapai (Photograph by George Wharton James, ca. 1880s, courtesy the Southwest Museum, Los Angeles)

in 1853 by another officer of the U.S. Corps of Topographic Engineers, Lieutenant Amiel Whipple, assigned to survey for a railroad across northern Arizona. Traveling along the general route of the present Santa Fe railroad, Whipple also missed seeing the Canyon. He was responsible, however, for naming Red Butte, that prominent landmark only a few miles from the South Rim.

In 1857, navy lieutenant Edward Beale, in an attempt to determine the feasibility of using camels as beasts of burden across the Great American Desert and to survey a wagon route, also passed along the same general route as had his two army predecessors.

It was not until 1857–1858 that the first official government expedition, under the command of Lieutenant Joseph Ives, actually visited the Grand Canyon. Ives had come some 350 miles up the Colorado River from its mouth in his small steamboat, *Explorer*. The river expedition ended when *Explorer* struck a rock and had to be abandoned. Lieutenant Ives and most of his men journeyed eastward, overland. Sometimes in the company of Walapai guides, sometimes without, he traveled to the bottom of the Grand Canyon at Diamond Creek and, later, into Havasu Canyon where at least one of his men, the German artist von Egglofstein, visited the Havasupai in their canyon home. Also with Ives was Dr. John Newberry, a geologist and the first scientist to study the Grand Canyon, or "Big Canyon," as Ives named it.

With increasing incursions into their territory, the Walapai and Havasupai became hostile toward Anglo-Americans and engaged in a bitter war with the U.S. Army from 1866 until their defeat in 1869. The United States established reservations for both tribes in 1882, ending forever their aboriginal life.

Lieutenant Joseph Christmas Ives's steamboat Explorer *on the lower Colorado in 1857, from a sketch by H. B. Mollhausen, artist for the expedition. (From Ives,* Report upon the Colorado River, *front.)*

North of the Grand Canyon, the Southern Paiute had suffered at the hands of mountain men, gold rush seekers, and emigrants alike along the Old Spanish Trail through southern Utah and Nevada. But the Paiute of the Kaibab band, living along the North Rim of the Grand Canyon and in its tributary canyons, were, for the most part, spared the atrocities of being shot at on sight or having their children stolen by slave traders. Their isolated position gave them some protection. The Mormons had made generally friendly contact with the Paiute in the 1850s and, by 1862, Mormon missionary and explorer Jacob Hamblin had traveled completely around the Canyon.

The early history of river running on the Colorado through the Grand Canyon will be treated later in this volume, but as a phase of exploration it will be summarized here. A man named James White claimed to have floated through the Canyon two years before the first recognized trip of Major John Wesley Powell. Recent research supports his claim even though his was not a historically documented exploration.

Powell, after his two river trips and subsequent geological and geographical explorations of the region immediately north of the Grand Canyon, influenced a number of other geologists and artists to study and paint the Grand Canyon. In the 1870s, noted American artist Thomas Moran, after having been in the field with Powell, prepared the illustrations for the major's 1875 report. In 1880, Moran accompanied Clarence Dutton, the geologist who had been in the field with Powell in 1875, to the canyon environs. William H. Holmes, an anthropologist and artist, prepared the drawings for Dutton's classic *The Tertiary History of the Grand Canon District* (with atlas), probably the most scholarly treatise of the Grand Canyon of the time and, today, the most exciting description that has ever been penned about the area.

Another geologist with Powell on the North Rim was Charles Walcott. The two of them engineered the construction of the Nankoweap Trail, built as usual upon ancient Indian foundations, off the North Rim in 1882 and 1883.

Prospecting for mineral wealth began in the Grand Canyon as early as the 1870s, as soon as the army assured peace with the Walapai and Havasupai. Eventually miners worked hundreds of claims for lead, zinc, copper, and asbestos.

Among the most notable were John Hance, William Bass, Louis Boucher, and Peter Berry. Hance established a camp on

The Kaibab Paiute reservation

the South Rim around the turn of the century and eventually
wound up telling tall stories at Grandview and, later, El Tovar
hotels. Meanwhile, he built trails into the Canyon off the South
Rim and developed asbestos mines near the rapid that bears his
name. Bass worked both copper and asbestos mines on both
sides of the river below Bass Point in the west central portion of
the Canyon about the same time. Boucher, the hermit of Hermit's Rest and Hermit Trail, lived at Dripping Springs and
worked copper deposits in Boucher Canyon. Berry, who helped
construct the Bright Angel Trail from 1890 to 1902, filed
claims on copper deposits on Horseshoe Mesa in the former

*Tailings and mine entrance at John
Hance's asbestos mine in the eastern Grand Canyon*

year. Later he managed the Grandview Hotel, constructed in
1897 near Grandview Point, the predecessor to the present-day
visitor accommodations at the Canyon.

Mining activities proved economically unprofitable shortly
after the turn of the century, and more of the miners turned
their attentions to the growing interest in tourism. In addition
to the Grandview Hotel, William Bass attracted tourists to his
camp at Bass Point, and J. W. Thurber, who operated the stage-
coach from Flagstaff to Grandview, constructed the first Bright
Angel Hotel.

By 1901, the Santa Fe railroad ran its track from Williams to
the Grand Canyon and, at a one-way fare of $3.95, put Thur-
ber's stage out of business. The famous El Tovar Hotel was constructed in 1905, as were the Hopi House, Babbitt's store, and
Verkamp's curio business. The future Grand Canyon Village
had begun where it is today, centered on El Tovar.

*A pre-1900 stage that ran from
Flagstaff to Grand Canyon*

Certainly the exploration period of the Grand Canyon had come to an end. Yet, as one examines the modern scientific record of studies—in anthropology, biology, ecology, geology— exploration continues in the tradition of many of the nineteenth-century scientists but equipped with twentieth-century ideas and techniques. May such exploration continue unabated into the twenty-first century and beyond.

SUGGESTED READING

Bolton, H. E.

  1949   *Coronado on the Turquoise Trail: Knight of Pueblos and
  Plains.* Albuquerque: University of New Mexico Press.

  1959   *Pageant in the Wilderness: The Story of the Escalante Expe-
  dition to the Interior Basin, 1776. Including the Diary and
  Itinerary of Father Escalante Translated and Annotated.* Salt
  Lake City: Utah State Historical Society.

Dutton, C. E.

  1882   *Tertiary History of the Grand Canon District* (with atlas).
  Washington, D.C.: GPO. Reprint. Salt Lake City: Peregrine Smith, 1977.

Garcés, F.

  1967   *A Record of Travels in Arizona and California, 1775–1776.*
  Translated and edited by John Galvin. San Francisco:
  John Howell.

Hughes, J. D.

  1978   *In the House of Stone and Light: A Human History of the
  Grand Canyon.* Grand Canyon: Natural History Association.

Ives, Joseph C.

  1861   *Report upon the Colorado River of the West.* Washington,
  D.C.: Government Printing Office.

James, G. W.

  1910   *The Grand Canyon of Arizona: How to See It.* Boston: Little Brown.

Manns, T.

  n.d.   *A Guide to Grand Canyon Village Historic District.* Grand
  Canyon: Natural History Association.

5 / *The Canyon by River*

KIM CRUMBO

*T*he morning sunlight casts a crimson hue on the cliffs surrounding Lees Ferry, the starting point for Grand Canyon river trips. Cool, moist air offers a moment's reprieve from the day's promised heat as river guides crawl from their sleeping bags to continue rigging and loading their boats. The morning's tranquillity lasts until trucks and buses arrive to unload gear and disgorge hordes of passengers on "the ramp" and the late morning sun begins to bake the rafters' boats, brains, and baggage.

River runners can be divided into three general groups: "privates," the people who outfit and operate their own trip; "commercial boaters," professional guides who conduct river tours for a fee; and "people," the folk who hire guides to take them down the river. The trip begins as boaters row or motor toward the east bank, avoiding the shallow water downstream. Visible on the shore are remnants of a trail ascending the low Moenkopi cliffs. This road, the Long Dugway, at one time allowed the passage of wagons and cars from the river crossing to the top of the Marble Platform before the construction of

Navajo Bridge ended the ferry's usefulness. A few minutes later the boat enters the Kaibab Formation, caprock of the Grand Canyon. "Kaibab," a Paiute word for "mountain lying down," gives a name to the plateau through which the Colorado River carved the eastern Grand Canyon. Here the river's thundering rapids inspire, terrorize, and sell profitable river trips that have in turn drastically changed the Canyon.

Today's boaters know that hundreds of thousands of fun-loving souls have survived Grand Canyon river trips, yet most sentient beings anticipate rapids with a mixture of dread and excitement. One can only imagine the thoughts of the first who followed the mysterious river, but the first documented river runner through the Canyon has left us his apprehension:

> We have an unknown distance to run, an unknown river to ex-
> plore. What falls there are, we know not. Ah well! We may conjec-
> ture many things. The men talk cheerfully as ever: jests are bandied
> about freely this morning, but to me the cheer is somber and the
> jests are ghastly.

That author, Major John Wesley Powell, found plenty of reasons for concern. In August of 1869, his was the first river party to reach the Grand Canyon. After surviving the Civil War (not to mention losing an arm in the battle of Shiloh) and having already endured six hundred dangerous miles of river, the Major faced not a wonderful whitewater adventure but the prospect of drowning or starving in the last great unknown region of the American West. Two and one-half months earlier, Powell and a crew of nine men had embarked from the small railroad town of Green River, Wyoming, to explore the generally unmapped and little-known regions drained by the Green and Colorado rivers.

Facing page 75: A pontoon raft in Lava Falls rapid

Though they learned much about the Colorado River, the months of leaking boats, lost supplies, musty flour, and plenty of coffee provided ample time to grow tired of river trips and each other. By the journey's end below the Grand Canyon, five men had abandoned the expedition (three of whom were subsequently killed, presumably by the Paiute), and the major had little solid scientific information to show for his tremendous efforts.

Despite this, the adventure assured Powell's fame. Most importantly, the United States supported him for a decade of exploring, mapping, geologizing, and studying the region's human inhabitants. In addition to scientific understanding, the major discovered something else:

> The Grand Canyon is a land of song. Mountains of music swell in the rivers, hills of music billow in the creeks, and meadows of music murmur in the rills that ripple over the rocks. Altogether it is a symphony of multitudinous melodies. All this is the music of waters.

He discovered that this harsh and dangerous desert canyon possesses aspects not simply interesting but inspirational as well. For music (as is its mirror image, beauty) is a human phenomenon. So is the Grand Canyon.

Powell certainly was not the first to descend into the Canyon; primitive hunters preceded him by at least 4,000 years. Likewise, the major may not have been the first to run the rapids. Undoubtedly some ancient Anasazi Basketmaker, intent upon a simple log-assisted river crossing, found himself blazing a route through President Harding, Shinumo, or North Canyon rapids. We will never know that frantic white-water pioneer, but history provides us with the name of one raftsman who

may have preceded Powell's expedition.

In September of 1867, residents of Callville, Nevada, pulled from the river a raving, sunburned man named James White. After a brief convalescence, he talked of prospecting in the San Juan River drainage with companions, of an Indian attack, and of an escape by river on a makeshift raft of rope and logs. One of his partners, Charles Baker, died in the ambush. Turbulent water unfortunately swept his other companion, George Strole, overboard in the rapids of the Colorado. After fourteen or more days of blazing sun and infrequent meals of mesquite seeds, lizards, and a leather knife scabbard, White washed out of the Canyon and launched a century of controversy.

Early river explorers encountered so much difficulty conducting organized expeditions that they could not believe (or admit) that a starving man, clinging to a makeshift raft, survived a journey through the "world's most dangerous river." Today, some experienced river runners believe the feat is possible, if not particularly enjoyable. Serious researchers tend to believe White's claim.

The unknown lured Powell to the Grand Canyon. His subsequent expeditions of scientists and artists produced not only maps, scholarly reports, and magnificent art but a Grand Canyon mystique as well.

Inevitably, men of different minds sought the river. In July of 1889, engineer Robert Stanton and Frank Mason Brown (president of the Denver, Colorado, Canyon and Pacific Railroad) led a party of six other men to attempt a survey along the river from western Colorado to the California desert below the Grand Canyon. They hoped to establish a water-level railroad to haul Colorado coal to West Coast markets.

An early-morning view of Isis Temple

Stanton wisely contacted Powell for advice on river expedi-

Robert Stanton's crew beginning their exploration of the Grand Canyon in 1889 (Photograph courtesy Miami University Library)

tions. The major suggested stout wooden craft similar to those used on his own expeditions and, most importantly, life jackets. Brown, in charge of outfitting the trip, foolishly provided cheaper light cedar boats and neglected to bring life jackets, an oversight that cost three lives. At Salt Water Wash, Brown's boat capsized and the president disappeared in the swirling water. The distraught crew waited the day in vain for the body to appear. Peter Hansbrough, a crew member, carved Brown's epitaph on the Supai ledges above the river. A few days later, Hansbrough and a black crewman, Henry Richards, perished in a similar manner at Twenty-five Mile Rapid. The survivors abandoned the expedition at South Canyon, but Stanton returned in December with stouter boats and lifejackets and completed the survey.

Fortunately, the railroad was never built.

The serious, perhaps somber, expeditions of Powell and Stanton publicized the Colorado and ushered in the era of river adventure for "any damn fool": "We must expect some accidents and expect to hit some rocks," wrote George Flavell, a boater and trapper from the calm waters of the lower Colorado River. "There is only one stone we must not hit . . . our tomb stone."

In 1896, Flavell convinced his future ex-friend Ramon Montez to accompany him on a grand adventure from Green River, Wyoming, to Yuma, Arizona. The crew's white-water experience began on that trip, with Flavell at the oars of the *Panthon* and Montez reluctantly perched on top of the duffel load. By Hance Rapid, Flavell's attitude on white-water boating had matured: he decided to portage. The river runners were unexpectedly surprised by three horsemen from the South Rim who approached the river and dismounted. With an audience on hand a surge of premature confidence and intrepidness filled their hearts. No one knows what filled their brains. Veteran river guide Amil Quayle once boasted, "Nobody ever accused a boatman of being intelligent." Flavell and Montez were about to prove him right.

In order to run the rapid successfully, they "had to make exact points," wrote Flavell, "which we failed to do." The *Panthon* slammed into a rock, and once they finally pried the boat free, it crashed from rock to rock—and completed the first documented run of Hance Rapid. Countless others have followed a similar course for similar reasons. Flavell and Montez continued their exploits to become the first to run all the rapids in the Grand Canyon except Soap Creek.

Flavell's ability to run all but one rapid marks an important development in white-water boating. Earlier river runners utilized flatwater techniques for rapid running. Oarsmen simply rowed downstream with their backs to the oncoming spectacle while a concerned tillerman did his best to avoid a disaster only he could see. Frederick Dellenbaugh, a member of Powell's second river expedition, described the procedure:

> I pulled the bow oars, and my back was toward the terrific roar which, like the voice of some awful monster, grew louder as we approached. It was difficult to refrain from turning around to see what it looked like now, but as everything depended on the promptness with which Hillers and I handled our oars in obedience to Powell's orders, I waited for the plunge, every instant ready to execute a command. . . . Then of a sudden there was a dropping away of all support, a reeling sensation, and we flew down the declivity with the speed of a locomotive. The gorge was in chaos. The boat rolled and plunged. The wild waters rolled over us, filling the open spaces to the gunwale.

This technique, exciting though it was, provided minimal control once the boat entered the rapid. Consequently, most river runners simply lined or portaged the formidable larger rapids. Lining involves the slow, tedious descent of a boat through a rapid by using lines controlled from shore. A portage involves carrying all gear and boats around the rapid. Either method involves hours of backbreaking effort.

Flavell discovered that by simply turning the boat around and running stern-first, he could see where he was going. It is surprising that the three previous expeditions failed to stumble

Russell's boat, wrecked in 1914 at the foot of Bass Trail

across this novel concept. At any rate, the technique allowed the boater a much better chance of negotiating the rapid since he could see the obstacles and avoid them—most of the time. Though Flavell was the first to utilize the stern-first method in the Grand Canyon, another important river runner, Nathaniel Galloway, probably developed the technique years earlier on the Green River in Wyoming and Utah.

By the turn of the century the Grand Canyon had evolved from an unknown "horrid abyss" to a national treasure. Powell explored its river. Clarence Dutton, Frederick Dellenbaugh, Powell, and others spoke eloquently of its beauty, vastness, and appeal. Artists such as William Holmes and Thomas Moran created not only inspirational representations of a natural wonder but an American art form as well. In 1903, President Theodore Roosevelt thundered:

> In the Grand Canyon, Arizona has a natural wonder which, so far as I know, is in kind absolutely unparalleled throughout the rest of the world. . . . Leave it as it is. You cannot improve on it. The ages have been at work on it, and man can only mar it. What you can do is to keep it for your children, your children's children, and for all who come after you, as the one great sight which every American . . . should see.

Within five years Roosevelt created Grand Canyon National Monument, and in 1919, Congress established Grand Canyon National Park. Publicity, the railroad, and a growing popularity of automobiles soon deluged the rims with curious tourists intent upon seeing the spectacle for themselves.

By comparison, the Colorado River seemed virtually unvisited and unknown. Hardy souls continued to ply the rapids, but they arrived in a trickle. Trappers and prospectors such as Nathaniel Galloway, William Richmond, and Benjamin "Hum" Wooley made way for Emery and Ellsworth Kolb, Charles Russell, and others hoping to profit from selling photographs, books, and motion pictures of their adventures. Engineers traversed the river in search of dam sites with which to harness the power of the Colorado.

In 1928, Bessie Hyde became the first woman to run the Grand Canyon's white-water. Her story ended tragically when she and her husband, Glen, disappeared below 232 Mile Rapid. Scientists of the Powell tradition returned in the Cal Tech-Carnegie Tech expedition of 1937–38, the same years Buzz Holmstrom became the first man to intentionally run the Canyon alone.

Until 1938, white-water boating remained within the realm of adventurous prospectors, scientists, and do-it-yourselfers. In that year, Norman Nevills conducted the first commercial river trip through the Grand Canyon. His clients included two women scientists whose botanical efforts began to describe the Canyon's flora. Until his untimely death in 1949, Norm conducted seven commercially guided trips in the Grand Canyon. Of the hundred people who boated the Canyon between 1869 and 1949, nearly one-third traveled with Nevills.

In the early 1950s, Georgie White, the first woman outfitter in the Grand Canyon, developed thirty-two-foot-long inflatable pontoon rafts that could haul twenty-six or more people downriver. The large craft required an outboard motor to maneuver. With the rising awareness of river running and the fancied safety of such trips, the Canyon became relatively popular. Between 1949 and 1954, another hundred people traversed the Canyon.

The pounding roar of 185-horsepower inboard motors ushered in the tumultuous 1960s. New Zealander Jon Hamilton led a flotilla of four jet boats upriver through the Grand Canyon in July of 1960. Three boats made it to Lees Ferry. During the decade that followed, the United States agonized over political assassinations, riots, and the war in Vietnam. It was also the darkest of times for the Grand Canyon.

Engineers designed and politicians supported the construction of several large hydroelectric dams within the Canyon. Marble Canyon Dam would have destroyed the river environment from mile 40 to a point upstream of Lees Ferry. Vaseys Paradise, numerous rapids, the Silver Grotto, Redwall Cavern, and a thousand other beautiful images would have drowned in the quiet depths of another Colorado River dam.

Bridge Canyon Dam would have inundated the lower Canyon. Lava Falls, Fern Glen, lower Havasu, and many more places would have been lost. These outrageous plans mobilized environmentalists, river runners, a few politicians, and other concerned human beings against the despoilers; the hydroelectric projects were killed (at least for now).

The dam debates generated nationwide interest in the Grand Canyon and the Colorado. As a result, the infant river-running industry experienced an explosive increase in clients. By 1967, the number of people traveling the river had increased to 6,000 each season. By 1972, that number had increased to 16,000, and commercial outfitters carried 90 percent of the traffic.

The condition of the river corridor was dismal. Human waste, toilet paper, charcoal from spent fires, and garbage seriously detracted from most of the once-pristine beaches used for camping. Crowding at once-secluded waterfalls, shady grottos, and ancient archaeological sites became a problem.

In response to public concern, the National Park Service imposed a ceiling on river use based on the 1972 use levels and soon initiated a series of scientific studies aimed at solving the problems. Park managers solved many of the serious effects such as human waste and trash accumulation by demanding that visitors simply carry the offending material out on the trip. They restricted fires and conducted revegetation projects each year to help restore areas damaged by wandering recreationists.

Other problems persisted. Even today, crowding remains a troublesome situation at popular attraction sites along the river. The noncommercial do-it-yourself rafters must wait years before their names appear at the top of a waiting list to boat the Canyon, while anyone with the money can find a space on a commercial trip at any time.

A view down Marble Canyon from the Nankoweap cliff granaries

In addition, the park service studies recommended the elimination of motorized boats. Motor proponents claimed, but failed to demonstrate, that the larger pontoon rafts were safer than the smaller oar-powered boats that carry four to six people. Oar-powered advocates insisted that the quiet non-motorized trips were much more relaxed, equally safe, and more in keeping with the wilderness environment of the Grand Canyon. At any rate, the larger craft carry three to five times the number of paying passengers, an economic incentive at the heart of the motor controversy. Although the extensive environmental and economic studies of the 1970s supported eliminating motors and adding controls to reduce congestion, a subsequent political battle forced the National Park Service to abandon this wilderness option.

How relevant is the wilderness option for the Colorado River in the Grand Canyon today? Wilderness presented early river runners with tremendous logistical problems that sometimes ended in starvation or death. Despite hardship and misery, the overwhelming and sometimes subtle beauty of untouched wilderness touched the mind and spirit of those who suffered most.

"The wonders of the Grand Canyon," wrote Powell,

A quiet stretch of the river in Marble Canyon

> cannot be adequately represented in symbols of speech itself. The resources of the graphic art are taxed beyond their powers in attempting to portray its features. The elements that unite to make the Grand Canyon the most sublime spectacle in nature are multifarious and exceedingly diverse. . . . Besides the elements of form, there are elements of color, for here the colors of the heavens are rivaled by the colors of the rocks. The rainbow is not more replete with hues. But form and color do not exhaust all the divine qualities of the Grand Canyon. It is the land of music.

The Colorado River's thundering rapids and busy riffles orchestrate Powell's music of waters on the grandest scale. The impatient boiling and swirl of the quieter sections and the chaotic tumble of the many side streams provide the Canyon's most subtle and charming aspects. Within the Grand Canyon there are many (but never enough) intriguing places. The most famous—Elves Chasm, Little Colorado River, Redwall Cavern, Deer Creek, Tapeats, and Havasu—are the most visited.

Quiet solitude is rare, particularly at Havasu Creek, except when winter transforms the once-brilliant green of Arizona grape and velvet ash into the stark, barren skeletons of dark vines and naked trees. Winter's cold shadows pervade the narrow canyon. A thousand small cascades create an endless chaos of blue water and white foam. Absent are the summer's bird calls, although an occasional canyon wren's melodic song cascades in harmony with the nearby stream. Absent is the warmth that invites the visitor to swim and stay. Absent, too, are the frequent whining aircraft and the summer crowds.

The wonders of the Grand Canyon are there for those willing to take the time and effort to travel by foot or boat, although a summer day might bring hundreds of people at any given time to one particular attraction. The visitor might find Powell's music of waters drowned by the drone of aircraft and outboard motors or trampled under the feet of the crowds. For now, winter's subfreezing temperatures offer the best chance for solitude. History has not ended, of course, and should the Park Service gain the necessary institutional courage (public support, in other words) to reduce noise and congestion, the best that the Canyon offers humanity will be there at any season.

The Grand Canyon consists of towering cliffs and buttes, of colorful or somber rocks, and of life from the majestic ponderosa pine to mysterious bighorn sheep to the smallest aquatic insects. The physical canyon is indeed the handiwork of nature, not man. Theodore Roosevelt beseeched us to "leave it as it is," knowing we can never "improve upon it," to ensure that future generations could discover for themselves what the great chasm evokes from the human heart and mind. Preservation of a natural environment for the benefit of mankind. The chance to gaze into the unspoiled depths of a gigantic chasm, or a quiet pool, and touch the essence of nature or the depth of human joy and sorrow. The Grand Canyon is, above all, the human response to an unspoiled natural wonder.

Powell understood: "The Grand Canyon is the land of song. All this is the music of waters."

SUGGESTED READING

Crumbo, K. H.
    1981   *A River Runner's Guide to the History of Grand Canyon.*
             Boulder, Colorado: Johnson Books.

Dellenbaugh, F. S.
    1926   *A Canyon Voyage.* New Haven: Yale University Press. Re-
             print. Tucson: University of Arizona Press, 1984.
    1965   *The Romance of the Colorado River.* Chicago: Rio Grande
             Press.

Eddy, C.
    1929   *Down the World's Most Dangerous River.* New York:
             Frederick A. Stokes.

Goldwater, B. M.
    1970   *Delightful Journey: Down the Green and Colorado Rivers.*
             Tempe: Arizona Historical Foundation.

Hamilton, J.
    1963   *Whitewater.* Christchurch, New Zealand: Caxton Press.

Hughes, D. J.
    1978   *In the House of Stone and Light: A Human History of the
             Grand Canyon.* Grand Canyon: Natural History Associa-
             tion.

Kolb, E. L.
    1914   *Through the Grand Canyon from Wyoming to Mexico.* New
             York: MacMillan Company. Reprint. Tucson: University
             of Arizona Press, 1989.

Lavender, D.
    1985   *River Runners of the Grand Canyon.* Grand Canyon: Natu-
             ral History Association. Reprint. Tucson: University of
             Arizona Press, 1989.

Nims, Franklin A.
    1962   *The Photographer and the River, 1889–1890: The Colorado
             Canyon Diary of Franklin Nims.* Edited by Dwight L.
             Smith. Santa Fe: Stagecoach Press.

Smith, Dwight L., and C. Gregory Crampton, eds.
    1987   *The Colorado River Survey: Robert B. Stanton and the Denver, Colorado Canyon & Pacific Railroad.* Salt Lake City and Chicago: Howe Brothers, 1987.
Stanton, Robert B.
    1968   *Down the Colorado.* Edited by Dwight L. Smith. Norman: University of Oklahoma Press.

6 / *Hiking the Canyon*

FRANK D. TIKALSKY

*H*umans have been at home in the Canyon with computer and spear; they have walked the Canyon barefoot and with Vibram soles. Strong evidence indicates that 4,000 years ago American Indians traveled the depths of the Canyon by foot in pursuit of game. Today, Grand Canyon National Park officials annually issue over 80,000 overnight hiking permits and estimate that during periods of heavy use approximately 400 persons daily hike the Bright Angel Trail.

The earliest visitors to the Grand Canyon did not seek recreation but rather the sustenance essential to life and, with an elegantly simple technology, apparently succeeded. Ironically, modern backpackers, aided by sophisticated paraphernalia, search for experiences common to their aboriginal predecessors, seeking relief from, rather than support for, technology. They seek escape from modernity, thus confirming Thoreau's observation that "we need to witness our own limits transgressed and some life pasturing freely where we never wander."

There is no better way to develop an appreciation for the

geology, ecology, and archaeology of the Canyon than by walking its depths. To fully appreciate the Canyon, the viewer requires both microscopic and macroscopic views, for there is no
other way to grasp its proportions. In a seven-hour walk from
the rim to the river, one penetrates six of the seven North
American life zones and descends through two-and-one-half
billion years of geologic time. No rim view can capture the excitement of these experiences. In twenty-five years of canyon
hiking below the rim, I have never experienced a minute for
which I have not been abundantly rewarded. To be sure, I still
do not grasp its dimensions; however, I am gaining a vast appreciation for its qualities.

The Canyon has provided me with leisurely hikes to places
of solitude and beauty as well as mountaineering challenges of
significant proportions. I have experienced solo hikes as well as
camaraderie with family and friends. Many mistakingly think of
canyon hiking as a trip to the bottom of an abyss. Not so.
There is much more varied adventure here than that. Some of
my most treasured memories are brief hikes to a special archaeological ruin, a secret spring, or a breathtaking vista.

Harvey Butchart, the famed canyon mountaineer and invet-
erate hiker, estimates that he has spent more than a thousand
days below the rim and has found more than a hundred routes
to the Colorado River—trails which Dr. Robert Euler, an expert
in Grand Canyon archaeology, believes were well-known to aboriginal explorers.

Thus, remember that the Canyon offers a variety of backpacking experiences ranging from relatively simple day-hiking
to challenging and demanding expedition outings that require
sound physical condition in addition to consummate skill in
backpacking and mountaineering. For any given trail, hikers

*Facing page 95: A mule train on
the South Kaibab Trail*

should thoroughly acquaint themselves with the demands of the hike, have the ability to cope with those demands, and make sure they have the appropriate equipment. Ignorance of these basic requirements has been fatal. (At the end of this chapter is a list of necessities considered basic for safe, comfortable backpacking in the Grand Canyon.)

Hikers unfamiliar with the Grand Canyon should know that many so-called trails are, for the most part, routes with only an occasional semblance of a trail. Thus, it is imperative to consult one or more hiking guidebooks (also listed at the end of this chapter) prior to attempting an inner canyon trek. The guidebooks by John Annerino and Stewart Aitchison are particularly valuable for people unfamiliar with the canyon environs. Anyone planning to negotiate the most commonly traversed unmaintained routes should consult Scott Thybony's guide. If, after becoming an experienced canyon hiker, you plan to attempt difficult, seldom-walked routes, you should familiarize yourself with the guides and articles by Harvey Butchart.

Many hiking guides evaluate Grand Canyon trails in terms of their difficulty and, on occasion, rank them. Be careful if you are unaware of the criteria used in such ratings. Do *not* accept trail-guide evaluations uncritically.

For example, guides frequently describe North Bass as the most difficult canyon trail, probably because of the obscureness of the route. If you consider obscureness the major criterion, such an estimation is probably correct; however, if dangerous exposure concerns you, some areas of the Nankoweap traverse would qualify as highly challenging. Always attempt to determine precisely the particular challenges and obstacles of a given trail and your ability to meet these challenges and obstacles.

An isolated Anasazi storage granary off the North Rim

How well do you read a map? Can you cope with exposure to heights? What is your level of physical conditioning?

Most hikes from the South Rim to the river involve an elevation change of 5,000 feet; those from the North Rim, 6,000 feet. Going downhill is often so deceptively simple that the evening ascent comes as a surprise to the weary traveler. All hikers share aching muscles and shortness of breath, but the poorly prepared have on occasion died or required rescue by helicopter or mule.

Though the Canyon is generally arid, the weather can be wet or dry, hot or cold. It rains, snows, and hails in the Canyon every year, and temperatures can vary from 20°F on the rim to 80°F at the river on the same day, with skiing on the rim and sunbathing at the river. Deep in the Canyon, freezing temperatures have been recorded in winter and the mercury has soared to 120°F in summer. The months of June through September are particularly hot; ordinarily, April and October provide ideal conditions for hiking.

Above all, safe hikers must carry ample supplies of water on any hike. Three quarts of water stored in separate plastic containers (sometimes containers leak) is a minimum requirement for any one-day trip below the rim. As a good rule of thumb, add one quart of water to the basic three-quart requirement for every ten degrees of temperature over 80°F. Thus, hiking for a six- to seven-hour period in hundred-degree temperatures requires at least five quarts of water. For safety, the hiker must be able to recognize symptoms of dehydration and heat fatigue.

Thirst is not always an accurate indication of dehydration, a fact particularly important for hikers who are in middle age or beyond. Drink water regularly and conservatively. Some hikers have become seriously dehydrated despite carrying ample water in their canteens!

Any introduction to Grand Canyon hiking would be incomplete if it did not address the most frequently asked question by uninitiated canyon hikers (What about the rattlesnakes?) and offer advice concerning the most frequently encountered problem (blisters).

Harvey Butchart estimates that if you tabulate the number of rock slides you hear and rattlesnakes you see over a long period of canyon hiking, their numbers will be few and almost equal. My canyon experience supports Butchart's assessment. Certainly my snake encounters have been few. I have more often seen scorpions, whose bite can be painful but generally not lethal for healthy adults. You can minimize rattlesnake and scorpion encounters by studying their characteristics prior to hiking the Canyon and being vigilant when the ambient temperature is approximately 70°F (especially at night). Always try to camp away from springs, underbrush, and rock walls. When you lift any flat object lying on the ground, do so by lifting the farthest end of the object first so that if a snake is beneath the object, it will be difficult for it to strike you. What do you do in the event of a rattlesnake bite? Medical opinion varies all the way from using tourniquets to instructing the victim simply to remain calm and consume fluids abundantly. Prepare for snakebites by consulting your physician before your trip. What he tells you to take should comprise your snakebite kit (some physicians advise against antivenin, for example).

Blisters, the most common problem encountered by all hikers, are something we can do a lot about. Stop at the first sign of foot discomfort and apply moleskin or "second skin." Wear two pairs of socks, with the inner one being silk. The problem called Grand Canyon toes, the worst canyon ailment, can also be lessened. I recently learned of the best precaution while backpacking in New Zealand. Hiking downhill for long periods can lead to very painful toe blisters. New Zealanders avoid this condition by packing the front of their boots with sheep's wool. This cushions their toes against the repeated toe trauma so common to extended downhill hiking.

After first walking the Bright Angel or the Kaibab, the novice hiker generally selects the Hermit, both because it is considered the "abandoned" trail that is least difficult and because it affords a location to obtain water enroute. Also, though a de-

Prehistoric Cohonina pictographs in Havasu Canyon dating from about A.D. 1100 (Photograph by Frank Tikalsky)

manding hike that requires negotiating rock-slide areas, it is the most heavily traveled of the nonmaintained trails and thus can be easily discerned. (Before attempting *any* inner canyon trail, please read at least one of the books listed at the end of this article.) Red Canyon, Tanner, Bass, and other unmaintained routes to the river are interesting and rewarding only if one has served an apprenticeship on the Hermit.

Hikers can access the Havasupai Reservation by walking either the Walapai or Topocoba trails, with the former being used by 99 percent of first-time visitors. Only the Havasupai Tribe grants the required permission to hike these trails. To contact the tribal reservation office, call (602) 445–2121 or write to Tourist Manager, Supai, AZ 86435.

You may obtain backcountry reservations for hiking in the national park only by writing the Backcountry Office or by appearing in person. The park service will provide all of the details needed to obtain a trip reservation, the rules applying to Grand Canyon hiking, and succinct information on trail difficulty from the Grand Canyon National Park 1988 Management Plan. Currently, beginning on October 1, the Backcountry Office will accept reservations for the following year. One may obtain reservation forms from Backcountry Office, Grand Canyon National Park, Grand Canyon, AZ 86023.

Individuals differ enormously in their psychological response to the Grand Canyon, and these idiosyncratic responses are amplified when one hikes below the rim. These responses affect how we hike, see, and interact with the Canyon.

Though psychological responses are only infrequently mentioned in Grand Canyon literature, some books present notable exceptions. Readers will find obvious examples in Colin Fletcher's chapter "Rock" in *The Man Who Walked Through Time* and Clarence Dutton's "The Panorama From Point Sublime" in *A Tertiary History of the Grand Canyon District*. Dutton, for example, observed,

> The lover of nature whose perceptions have been trained elsewhere will enter this strange region with a shock, and dwell there for a time with a sense of oppression. The bold will seem grotesque, the colors too bizarre, the subtlety absent. But time will bring a gradual change, and the strength and majesty will come through. Great innovations, whether in art or literature, in science or in nature, seldom take the world by storm. They must be understood before

they can be estimated, and they must be cultivated before they can be understood.

Personal psychological meanings garnered in Grand Canyon hiking vary enormously. An American writer is said to have exclaimed (upon seeing the Canyon for the first time), "There goes God with His flags unfurled." On the other hand, one tourist exclaimed to a woman I assumed to be his wife, "Did you bring me all the way from Detroit simply to see this?"

Famed psychologist Carl Jung thought in terms of four personality types, which he classified on the basis of psychological functions: thinking, feeling, sensing, intuiting. These functions sometimes help me understand the psychological manner in which the hiker experiences the Canyon. For example, when Jung's feeling function is dominant, the person fills with awe and a sense of grandeur. When the sensation function is predominant, visual impact is foremost, and the person experiences the Canyon as a striking, colorful photograph. Those focused on the thinking function have a strong inclination to become enamored with principles of geology and theoretical dynamics. And for the intuitive comes sense of meaning that transcends the immediate, profoundly mystical in nature. Your experience in hiking the Grand Canyon will certainly put you in touch with some and perhaps elements of all these experiences. You will find, I believe, that the Grand Canyon has a special way of allowing you to examine introspectively some of your deepest feelings and thoughts.

Aside from Jungianism, observers see more mundane psychological types: environmentalists, tree huggers, athletes, artists, photographers, bird watchers, amateur archaeologists, and biologists. All sorts of people with varying values and beliefs find unique meaning here. Indeed, if anything approaches the awesomeness of the Canyon, it is the human response to it. A Grand Canyon hike is, in a sense, one way to learn about your-self. In this sense, you must find your own psychological route.

There are also practical psychological aspects to canyon hik-ing. Experienced hikers and climbers recognize that in the out-of-doors our perceptions of time, distance, and size are often distorted. In my wilderness experiences nowhere is this more true than in the Grand Canyon, and sometimes these distor-tions can create difficulty.

A view of the Colorado River from the rim some seven to ten miles away and five to six thousand feet below leaves one with the perceptual illusion that the Canyon can't be that deep nor the river that far away. Conversely, psychological studies of per-ception show a strong tendency for us to lengthen the vertical line in any horizontal-vertical line relationship ($\perp$). Thus, those on the bottom of the Canyon tend to perceive the rim as much higher than it actually is. (Interestingly, my own professional research indicates that this tendency is significantly less in the Havasupai who live in the Canyon.)

These perceptual distortions have crucial implications in canyon backpacking. In groups I have led, hikers tend to un-derestimate the difficulty in going downhill and correspond-ingly overestimate the difficulty in going uphill. The latter tendency frequently generates hiker anxiety and causes the per-son to adopt a pace that is often much too fast.

For example, a number of years ago I took my then-four-year-old son on a hike from the North to the South Rim. We began our hike out of the Canyon at Phantom Ranch at about five in the morning, and at about six AM my son began count-ing hikers who were passing us. By seven AM perhaps two

A prehistoric defensive structure on an "island" off the South Rim

dozen persons (some of whom were almost jogging) had passed us. And then the inevitable. Very soon my son began counting hikers we passed. When we emerged on the rim shortly before noon we had passed all but two or three of the hikers who had earlier passed us. Ours had been a slow, steady pace. Most of those who passed us in the early morning hours were, I believe, inexperienced hikers driven by their anxiety and not an accurate appraisal of either trail difficulty or aerobic fitness. They were, at least in part, victims of perceptual illusion.

Similarly, in going downhill, inexperienced hikers will often start out at almost a trot and by the time they reach the river they have sore toes, ankles, and knees. In contrast, when experienced hikers descend long distances they do so slowly and in a fashion sometimes referred to as the mountaineering waddle: the person rocks back and forth like a duck to absorb downhill stress in the calf and quadriceps muscles instead of the knees, ankles, and toes. This may seem a foolish maneuver for those who believe the bottom of the Canyon is only a short distance away.

Another distortion involves the perception of a trail at some distance. Because of a lack of perspective, trails often appear to lie on precipitous shelves when in fact the trail is quite wide and has only minimal exposure.

One may combat these distortions by concentrating on small segments of the hike, maintaining a reasonable pace, and being aware of the distortions.

Fatigue and dehydration may also impair judgment and mood. Lost hikers have been found without shoes and have even abandoned their packs which contain the very supplies needed for survival. To avoid these problems, hikers must maintain a modest pace, consume water frequently, and rest regularly.

Not all who visit the canyon depths find world-shaking insights or understanding, but most of us acquire new perspectives and enormous aesthetic enrichment. Some of us also feel we have gained a sense of oneness with others who have walked there from aboriginal times to the present. True, the Canyon imposes harsh conditions on those who descend below the rim: Nature, they say, is a hanging judge, but treat her well, obey her rules, and all will go well. Become intimate with the

A view from the mouth of Stanton's Cave (Photograph courtesy Paul Long)

Grand Canyon, and you will be rewarded in ways that will boggle your mind.

Articles considered necessary for safety and comfort in Grand Canyon backpacking:

1. Comfortable, well-worn hiking boots in excellent condition
2. Four 1-quart plastic water bottles
3. Two plastic garbage bags (for covering pack in case of rain and for carrying out trash)
4. Extra wool socks
5. One pair long pants
6. One pair shorts
7. Lightweight wool sweater or shirt
8. Lightweight wind shirt
9. Lightweight poncho
10. Hat for sun cover
11. Metal cup and spoon
12. Bivouac cover and ground cloth or tent
13. Lightweight mattress
14. Lightweight sleeping bag:
    2 lb. down for fall and summer
    2-1/2 lb. down for winter
15. Sunscreen
16. Sunglasses
17. Insect repellent
18. Moleskin (for blisters)
19. Backcountry stove (campfires not allowed)

TRAILS
(U.S. Geological Survey maps are listed for trails below the rim.)

RIM TRAILS / South

Rim Trail. A 4-mile walk that follows the rim of the Canyon from Yavapai Museum to Maricopa Point. As a suggestion, view the interpretive programs at Yavapai Museum before walking the trail.

RIM TRAILS / North

Bright Angel Point Trail. A 1/3-mile self-guided nature trail that begins at trailside near Grand Canyon Lodge.

Transept Canyon Trail. A leisurely 1-1/2-mile trail along the rim from Grand Canyon Lodge to North Rim Inn and Campground.

Widforss Trail. One of the most rewarding of the rim trails, 10 miles round-trip. Outstanding vistas.

Cape Royal Trail. A 1/3-mile self-guiding nature trail from the Cape Royal Parking lot.

MAINTAINED TRAILS / South

Bright Angel Trail (15′ Bright Angel, Arizona). This is part of the longest route to Phantom Ranch. It is 8 miles from the trailhead near the Kolb Studio to the rest house at the Colorado River. There is water at Indian Gardens, 4.4 miles from the rim. During the *summer* there is water at two rest houses which are 1.5 and 3.3 miles from the rim.

Kaibab Trail (15′ Bright Angel, Arizona). Trailhead is 4.5 miles east of Grand Canyon Village. A steep, 6.5-mile waterless route to the Colorado River. This is the shortest maintained route to the river.

River Trail (15′ Bright Angel, Arizona). It is 1.8 miles from the river rest house at the bottom of Bright Angel Trail to the Kaibab Trail junction near the old suspension bridge. It is 1 mile from the trail junction to Phantom Ranch.

MAINTAINED TRAILS / North

North Kaibab Trail (15′ Bright Angel, Arizona). This is a 14-mile trail starting at the North Rim and ending at the suspension bridge at the Colorado River. Water is relatively plentiful after one descends through the Redwall. This is the only maintained trail from the North Rim to the river.

UNMAINTAINED TRAILS / South

Tonto Trail (15′ Bright Angel, Arizona). A trail that traverses the side canyons of the Grand Canyon on the south side of the Canyon, from Garnet Canyon on the west to Red Canyon on the east. Seldom walked for its own sake, this is regarded as a connecting trail. The portion of the trail between Hermit and Kaibab used to be maintained.

Dripping Springs Trail (15′ Bright Angel, Arizona). A 3-mile hike to Hermit Basin. There is ample water at Dripping Springs.

Hermit Trail (15′ Bright Angel, Arizona). An excellent introduction to inner-canyon, abandoned-trail hiking. Trail is in fair condition. Santa Maria Spring is dependable. Approximately 7 miles to Hermit Camp, 8 miles from rim to the river.

Boucher Trail (15′ Bright Angel, Arizona). Trailhead is south of Mesa Eremita, but most hikers connect with Boucher by walking Hermit to Dripping Springs Trail. Descending through the Hermit-Supai formation is difficult. This is not a trail for beginners or those unfamiliar with topographic map reading.

Grandview-Horseshoe Mesa trails (15′ Vishnu Temple, Arizona). Begins at Grandview Point and descends to the Tonto Plateau 3 miles below. Several spur trails are found on the Tonto Plateau.

New Hance Trail (Red Canyon). Trailhead is 1 mile west of Moran Point turnoff in a shallow drainage. This is a waterless, difficult, scenic 8 miles to Hance Rapids. Redwall descent must be found.

South Bass Trail (15′ Havasupai Point). Trailhead is 4 miles north of Pasture Wash. The road from Grand Canyon Village to Pasture Wash is in poor condition. Trail above Redwall is sometimes hard to find.

UNMAINTAINED TRAILS / North

Clear Creek Trail (15′ Bright Angel, Arizona). This is a 9-mile trail from Phantom Ranch to Clear Creek. It is waterless until one reaches Clear Creek.

Thunder River Trail (15′ Powell Plateau, Arizona). Trailhead is at Indian Hollow, 18.3 miles southwest of the Forest Ranger Station at Big Springs. It is a 13-mile trip to Thunder River and Tapeats Creek.

North Bass (Shinumo) Trail (15′ Powell Plateau, Arizona, and 15′ Havasupai Point, Arizona). Trailhead is at Swamp Point, which is 20 miles west of North Rim entrance station. It is 14 miles to the Colorado River.

Nankoweap Trail (15′ Nankoweap, Arizona). Trailhead is located in the saddle below Saddle Mountain. This is a long, dry trail, which ultimately follows Nankoweap Creek to the river.

TRAILS TO HAVASUPAI

There are several very difficult trails to the Havasupai Village that are not maintained, and their use is strictly forbidden by the tribe. Trails that may be used with tribal permission are the Walapai and Topocoba trails.

SUGGESTED READING

Aitchison, S.

1968   Elve's chasm. *Summit* 12(10):2–5.

1975   A Grand Canyon trek around the thumb. *Summit* 21(7):10–13.

1976   Human impact on the Grand Canyon. *Down River* 3(2):18–19.

1977   The Grand Canyon is a world in itself. *Plateau* 49(4): 3–9.

1982   Footprints in the Canyon. *Summit* 28(6):11–14.

1985   *A Naturalist's Guide to Hiking the Grand Canyon.* Englewood Cliffs, New Jersey: Prentice-Hall, Inc.

Annerino, J.

1986   *Hiking the Grand Canyon.* San Francisco: Sierra Club Books.

Butchart, H.

1962   Old trails in the Grand Canyon. *Appalachia* 28(7):45–64.

1964   Backpacking Grand Canyon trails. *Summit* 10(5):12–19.

1968   Routes into Grand Canyon's remote upper corner. *Summit* 14(2):22–28.

1970   *Grand Canyon Treks.* Glendale, California: La Siesta Press.

1973   Grand Canyon's Enfilade Point route. *Summit* 19(5):18–21.

1975   *Grand Canyon Treks II.* Glendale, California: La Siesta Press.

1976   Summits below the rim. *Journal of Arizona History* 17(1):21–38.

1984   *Grand Canyon Treks III.* Glendale, California: La Siesta Press.

Thybony, S.

1980   *A Guide to Hiking the Inner Canyon.* Grand Canyon: Natural History Association.

ABOUT THE CONTRIBUTORS

Dr. Stanley S. Beus, who has a Ph.D. degree from the University of California at Los Angeles, is Regents Professor of Geology at Northern Arizona University in Flagstaff. He has been conducting research in the Grand Canyon for some twenty-five years.

Dr. Steven W. Carothers, who has a Ph.D. degree from the University of Illinois, is a noted zoologist who has published extensively on Grand Canyon ecology. His most recent book, written with Dr. Bryan Brown, is *The Colorado River Through Grand Canyon: Natural History and Human Change,* published by the University of Arizona Press. Dr. Carothers is President of SWCA, Inc., Environmental Consultants in Flagstaff, Arizona.

Kim Crumbo is a National Park Service ranger and a boatman in the Division of Resource Management at Grand Canyon National Park. He has been a boatman on numerous river trips through the Grand Canyon and has published *A River Runner's Guide to the History of Grand Canyon.*

Dr. Robert Euler is a professional anthropologist with a Ph.D. degree from the University of New Mexico. He has been conducting research in the Grand Canyon since 1956 and has published numerous studies of his work on Grand Canyon archaeology and history, and with the American Indians of the area.

Dr. Frank Tikalsky is a psychologist on the clinical staff of the Los Alamos National Laboratory in New Mexico. He holds an Ed.D. degree from Northern Colorado University in Greeley. He has hiked extensively over most of the maintained trails as well as many little-used trails in the Grand Canyon, has published research on Grand Canyon history, and has conducted psychological studies among the Havasupai Indians who live in the Grand Canyon.

Ann Zwinger is a noted natural history author and a veteran of several river trips through the Grand Canyon.